KATRINA
WAS BIG
BUT GOD IS
BIGGER

ST. CLARE PARISH

"It will get better, and we need all the wonderful help we are getting from everybody all over the country, and one day we will be able to reciprocate."

—Pam West, Bay St. Louis, Mississippi

CONTENTS

ACKNOWLEDGEMENTS

When a book comes to life, it is always due to the incredible team of people who have worked together creating a logical way to tell the story and paint the picture from the eyes of the visionary. This book, in particular, shares a vision—from a set of real circumstances—that is dear to the hearts of many who live in the Gulf Coast and want to return home. I am so blessed to have shared a life experience with the wonderful families in the Gulf Coast, for it is their stories that bring this message to you and to everyone across the planet as we reach out asking for your help to rebuild a community of friends and families. Thank you to all of my friends in Mississippi. You are so very special, and I am so blessed to have met you.

A special thank you to Bobby Ingram for all of your hard work, information and tireless hours of perseverance. I look forward to many more Gulf Shrimp dinners.

To all of the builders, modular home companies, city officials, city staff and contractors, without whom nobody would be able to return home.

A very special thank you to my friend and associate, Bob Yehling, without whom I never would have been able to share this incredibly inspirational project. You are the best and I am blessed; thank you!

To Governor Haley Barbour, who has done an amazing job moving the redevelopment of the State of Mississippi forward.

DEDICATION

To every investor who sees the vision of the Gulf Coast and invests from the heart, may your pockets be as filled with profit as your heart is full with love.

INTRODUCTION

In my book, *The Casual Millionaire*, I wrote two chapters that seemed to have in mind the redeveloping Gulf Coast and the enormous opportunity presented by the Gulf Opportunity Zone Act: "Location! Location! Location!" and "The Big Win." One is a vital strategy and the other a vital mind-set for anyone who's interested in writing his or her own financial success story. In my own successful real estate career, I have seen very few opportunities that so completely marry these two concepts than the rebuilding of the Gulf Coast. The federal government has created a win-win situation for all parties (builders, realtors, investors, tenants, homebuyers) in a very specific location. I couldn't have dreamed up a better real estate scenario for any of my books that combined the perfect location and the right timing with an opportunity like this to win big!

But, much as it would make for a truly serendipitous moment, I wasn't thinking about *The Casual Millionaire* or how the Gulf Coast would play into my work during late August and early September 2005. Like most other Americans, I was horrified and riveted by what Hurricane Katrina and the resulting breach of the levee along Lake Pontchartrain had wrought in New Orleans and the surrounding Gulf Coast. One thought I had as my heart leapt out to the hundreds of thousands of displaced people was, "What if they didn't use the equity of their homes as capital to invest in other real estate or pension funds or the stock market and instead put everything into paying down the thirty-year mortgages?"

Even now, my stomach sinks when I ponder the question. Most of the people who lost their homes in New Orleans and in the Texas, Mississippi, Louisiana, and Alabama Gulf coasts to Hurricanes Katrina and Rita—the latter of which struck three weeks later in Texas and Louisiana—did not put their equity to further use. When they lost their homes, they lost everything! The financial and emotional damage was made worse for many homeowners when it turned out their homeowners' policies might have covered *either* the hurricane *or* the flood unleashed by the levee break a day later, but not *both*. Thus, many did not receive the settlements they anticipated. They left their hometowns of New Orleans, Metairie, Mobile, Bay St. Louis, and other places in more than a hundred counties, leaving behind perhaps generations of family roots and walking into an uncertain future with a $2,000 credit card from the Federal Emergency Management Agency (FEMA). Within a few weeks, New Orleans and the surrounding areas had seen their prehurricane population reduced by more than 50 percent, creating the most massive exodus of displaced humans from a natural disaster in U.S. history.

That led to a few questions many people, including me, asked: How are government officials going to get these people back home? How many of them will return home? And who is going to do the rebuilding?

Certainly, I knew that for the rebuilding, the government would involve the private and business sectors to some degree. After all, no government is equipped or funded to rebuild hundreds of thousands of homes, business structures, industrial park complexes, municipal buildings, restaurants, shops, and other establishments.

I watched the aftermath of Hurricanes Katrina, Rita, and then Wilma—which sideswiped southern Florida in October 2005—with keen interest on a number of levels. As a former Air Force officer, I knew what it took to quickly mobilize large groups of people, as the government was doing with the National Guard and as relief organizations were doing on the ground. As a woman, my heart went out to the hundreds of thousands of people directly impacted by the hurricane. As a real estate agent and developer, I wondered how soon the primary cleanup could be completed and the rebuilding commence, and who would be allowed to participate in the rebuilding. Would it only be locals, in-state residents, or out-of-state parties such as me?

And, as a citizen who possesses a deep confidence in this nation's resourcefulness and capacity for overcoming disaster, I grew keenly interested in how the government would respond to the long rebuilding process that lay ahead. The Bush administration was well-known for placing much of the economic growth of the country in the hands of the biggest and most motivated drivers: the businesses and individuals who used their capital to invest, build, generate businesses and jobs, and build some more. I knew the federal government would do something, but when and how soon?

The answer came in the form of a program that has occupied much of my professional life and generated much enthusiasm within me in the past two years: the Gulf Opportunity (GO) Zone Act, known in Congress as House Resolution 4440. Passed in December 2005, the GO Zone Act makes it possible for builders, developers, and qualified real estate agents to rebuild designated areas and lease them back to displaced local residents, who then can purchase the homes within five years of moving in. Thanks to well-integrated programs between the federal government and state initiatives such as the one I'm particularly familiar with, the Mississippi Development Authority, outside real estate investors can obtain a potentially forgivable loan from the state. They can have homes built, then managed by a licensed property management company such as my company, A-Shore-Bet Property Management, LLC. After one year, they receive a 50 percent bonus home depreciation of up to a $100,000 direct tax deduction of adjusted gross income for that tax year for a single $200,000 home! They will help a family return home in the process.

Then, sometime within five years, after receiving rental income to wholly or partially offset the mortgage, and still claiming the standard depreciation *after* receiving the initial 50 percent bonus home depreciation, the investor can sell the home to the family at its original sale price.

Sound like one of the best real estate opportunities you've heard of? Well, let me catch my breath for a moment, because there's more! An individual, corporation, limited liability corporation, or partnership group can purchase up to five new homes in the GO Zone. The buyer can utilize up to four entities for buying new homes; thus, the buyer can potentially obtain these remarkable tax breaks, allowances, and incentives for twenty properties, which we manage for them. In addition, if the buyer is interested in repairing or reconstructing damaged homes, he or she can purchase up to twenty such homes per entity. This is a prime example of what I will present in my next book, *The Quantum Millionaire*: a golden opportunity to go quantum with an investment. I will always be the first to tell you to physically set foot on any ground or in any home you intend to purchase and also the first to recommend that you work with a property-management company to manage your units when you're dealing from out-of-state. In this case, it's also required.

When I first heard about the Gulf Opportunity Zone Act, I became excited enough to check it out thoroughly. When I researched the act, contacted officials in the affected states, learned about the requirements for operating within the states and the regulations of the acts, and understood the magnitude of building needed to restore the Gulf Coast, I did what I always do when a great and meaningful opportunity comes along: I jumped on it! I told my staff, partners, and others in the business, "This is the greatest tax incentive that's come along in my lifetime!" It won't be the last time you hear me make this statement in this book, and in *Investing in the GO Zone*, I will lay out all the specifics of what I mean.

Once I learned the parameters of working within the GO Zone, I began to secure properties to offer for development, the largest of which will house 9,700 homes near Bay St. Louis, Mississippi, one of the hardest-hit communities. I also created a series of seminars in California, Arizona, Nevada, and other states to educate potential investors on the GO Zone and the incredible tax and financial advantages of participating in this profitable mission. These seminars are also available online at our official GO Zone website, www.thegozoneconnection.com. I will continue to lead seminars and field trips to the GO Zone, because time is of the essence: following a time extension announced last year, the benefits of this act will run out at the end of 2010 in Mississippi and Louisiana, and at the end of 2009 in Alabama.

That's another point that I try to illustrate in this book, that you often do not see "profit" and "mission" used in the same sentence, but in this case, you bet you do—just ask any longtime Gulf Coast resident who was able to return home from a temporary out-of-state residence, FEMA trailer, rented apartment, or relative's house because an outside investor created a home under the Gulf Opportunity Zone Act. Within five years, that individual and his or her family can own that house. In their eyes and the eyes of thousands of others who are in the same boat, we GO Zone investors are Samaritans of a high order. And this scenario comes with great financial incentive for us. What could be a more win-win situation than this?

In *Investing in the GO Zone*, I provide a complete picture of the Gulf Opportunity Zone Act and why it might well be the best real estate investment. I share stories of people affected by the storms and of their hopes and dreams that enabled state and federal officials to develop such a great program for returning Gulf Coast residents to their homeland. I also break down the particulars of the GO Zone Act, the tax incentives and advantages for investors and builders, and how we're developing these properties. I further lay out the necessity of working through a qualified and well-positioned property management company such as A-Shore-Bet, how to begin the investment process through our website, www.thegozoneconnection.com, and some things to watch out for when looking into investing in the GO Zone.

My team and I have supplemented *Investing in the GO Zone* with our official website, www.thegozoneconnection.com. It provides up-to-the-minute updates on our work in the GO Zone, photos and videos from the area, seminar schedules, copies of governmental forms, and pamphlets referenced in this book, such as IRS Publication 4492, which details the tax particulars of the Gulf Opportunity Zone Act, and much more. Visit us.

Not often does a single real estate opportunity prompt the creation of a book, but this is such a great opportunity that I wanted to make sure every possible investor knew about it and received com-

plete information so he or she could act quickly. I am so excited and certain about this program and our ability to assist the investors to achieve their goals within it that I could have easily subtitled this book *Unparalleled Loss, Unequalled Opportunity.*
Let's visit the GO Zone!

Tonja Demoff
April 2008

CHAPTER

1

On The Ground

It was a natural disaster unlike any other, with damage to property and lives that continues to impact the Gulf Coast and the nation years later.

Out of the Gulf of Mexico roared a Category 5 hurricane so large that its cloud mass exceeded the square mileage of Texas. More than 1.2 million people living along the Louisiana, Mississippi, Alabama, and Florida panhandle coasts were given mandatory evacuation orders. Emergency operation centers were activated and prepositioned supplies readied for an anticipated region-wide cutoff from essential services. For the first time ever, the National Weather Service issued a warning through its New Orleans/Baton Rouge office that predicted the area would be "uninhabitable for weeks" after "devastating damage." In retrospect, that dire forecast was optimistic.

After spinning ominously off the Louisiana coast and apparently locked on a bull's-eye course for New Orleans, Katrina initially jogged slightly northeast. The outer delta parishes suffered first, experiencing near-complete destruction from winds, high seas, torrential rains, and flooding. New Orleans faced hundred-mile-per-hour winds, but fortunately for the Crescent City, the hurricane showed only its western side—the weaker side—as it moved past. On August 29, 2005, when Katrina made landfall, New Orleans was not initially the worst-hit area; the Mississippi coast was. Katrina delivered a direct hit, its greatest storms quickly swamping the low-lying area with twenty-foot waves and a tidal surge that raced more than a mile inland. Winds exceeding 130 miles per hour tore apart whatever remained. Two cities lying on the Hancock County peninsula between the Gulf of Mexico and St. Louis Bay—Waveland and Bay St. Louis—suffered near-total losses. Just east of Hancock County, one of the I-10 bridges spanning Alabama's wide Mobile Bay suffered serious structural damage when a drifting oil barge rammed into its supports, cutting off critical eastbound access.

It couldn't possibly get worse.

But it did.

In the middle of the night, New Orleans residents slept after breathing a sigh of relief over the fact that a feared Category 5 strike had only delivered Category 2 winds and rain instead. Then catastrophe struck. The levees holding back the waters of the massive Lake Pontchartrain breached in fifty-three places, and the Mississippi River Gulf Outlet breached in twenty places. For the next twenty-four hours, the flooded lake and the overfilled river poured into all parts of the city east of the Mississippi, as well as into the neighboring St. Bernard Parish, until the water level on both sides of the breached levees achieved equilibrium. Entire wards and districts were submerged beneath up to twelve feet of water. Worst of all, the water could not recede or be pumped out or diverted until the water levels on Lake Pontchartrain and the Mississippi dropped.

Given the amount of rainfall and the geography of the low-lying area, nothing could be done for days, days that seemed like months in the interminable late-summer heat and humidity. The worst-case scenario that Louisiana and federal officials had warned residents against and tried to prepare for for years was at hand: 80 percent of New Orleans was underwater.

Over the next week, all of us watched in eerie, horrified fascination as the tragedy played out. Nearly all of New Orleans' population was displaced. More than half never returned home. Tens of thousands of structures were either flooded or destroyed. More than one thousand people died. Entire hospitals failed; banks lost cash and depositor records; police precincts were rendered useless; tourists were stranded in the upper floors of downtown hotels; court records for everything from criminal cases to tax payments were lost; thirty oil platforms were destroyed; and 24 percent of the nation's annual oil production and 18 percent of its gas production was shut off for six months, sending prices skyrocketing at pumps nationwide. The entire infrastructure of New Orleans and many surrounding communities ceased to exist. An entire economic engine stopped. In the last week of August, more than four hundred thousand people lost everything they owned, and, if their home mortgage payments had served as the entirety of their investments, they lost all of their net asset value as well.

Two years after the storm, New Orleans' population remained at two hundred thousand people below its pre-Katrina level. Most of the displaced residents resettled in Houston, Mobile, Baton Rouge, Hammond, and other southern cities, though some relocated as far away as Seattle, Minneapolis, and Boston. As I watched this displacement, I wondered:

When will these people come home?

What will bring them home?

What will they come home to?

What can be done to offer them something besides FEMA trailers to encourage their return and, in doing so, restore their pride and sense of self-worth?

New Orleans became the focal point for global media coverage of Hurricane Katrina's onslaught. The hopelessness on the faces of people of all ethnic and socioeconomic backgrounds will remain in our memories forever. The sight of tens of thousands of people converging on the Louisiana Superdome will always be an icon of Katrina. The initial response of government officials will continue to be questioned, even though, if we think about it, they were in the same boat as the rest of us: astonished, overwhelmed, grasping for immediate fixes to stop the suffering. After dispatching FEMA to coordinate immediate disaster relief and the National Guard to restore order, the government appropriated a mind-boggling $116 billion in a series of relief bills (about half of the money had been utilized as of August 2007). Next, the Congress and the Bush administration went right to work on a greater response, the private investment aspect, which is the subject of this book.

However, New Orleans was not alone in its suffering, not by a long shot. From Port Charles, Louisiana, to Apalachicola Bay, Florida, and extending inland more than 150 miles, damage from Katrina and its storm surge was severe. Katrina was so widespread that it retained tropical storm force until it reached Clarksville, Tennessee, more than 500 miles north! Three weeks later, Hurricane Rita dealt a second crippling blow to the western Louisiana parishes and to eastern Texas. Then, a month after that, Hurricane Wilma laid siege to the southern and southwest Florida coasts. All of this occurred just one year after four separate hurricanes had carved up coastlines and laid claim to federal emergency dollars throughout the south. Taken together, a coastline longer than that of California now looked like the impact zone from a bombing mission. While the media continued to focus on the greater New Orleans area, more than two million people throughout the Gulf Coast tried to answer a single question: how do I rebuild my life and regain what I worked so hard to own?

That is where I decided to step in and to invite you along.

Back to Mississippi

While the New Orleans area lay submerged beneath the flood-waters wrought by Katrina's storm surges and rainfall, the folks along the Mississippi and Alabama coasts contended with an equally life-changing disaster. The eye wall of Katrina, which missed New Orleans, passed over the Hancock County cities of Waveland and Bay St. Louis, killing fifty-five people and washing away thousands of homes and businesses. The eye wall retained hurricane strength until it passed over Meridian, Mississippi, more than 150 miles inland. Waters from the massive twenty-eight-foot storm surge wiped out everything in its path for up to *six miles* inland. At one point, more than half of Hancock County was underwater, completely destroying Waveland and almost completely destroying Bay St. Louis and its delightful, historic downtown area, a strong source of tourism as well as local dollars. Later, it was determined that the twenty-eight-foot storm surge was the largest in recorded U.S. history!

Structures fortunate enough to escape the surge fell to the winds and the aftermath of ten inches of rain, replaced by bridges, barges, boats, piers, cars, and debris from half-dozen floating casinos that the hurricane had swept inland. The Bay St. Louis-Pass Christian and Biloxi-Ocean Springs bridges were destroyed; it took twenty months to complete rebuilding the Bay St. Louis-Pass Christian Bridge. The eastbound span of the I-10 bridge over the Pascagoula River estuary was damaged, limiting crucial east-west interstate traffic to two lanes for many weeks. Because most of the visitors and businessmen came to Hancock County from the east, the loss of the Bay St. Louis-Pass Christian Bridge virtually stopped business.

According to Mississippi officials, 90 percent of all structures within half a mile of the coastline were completely destroyed. Almost 9,000 FEMA trailers were occupied by Hancock County families, and nearly 27,000 county residents received additional FEMA assistance. The Mississippi Department of Forestry estimated that 1.3 million acres of prime forest lands were destroyed. More than 900,000 people statewide lost power, as did over two million others in Louisiana, Alabama, and western Florida.

Although the immediate impact of Katrina was devastating, the long-term effects left many thousands feeling helpless and hopeless in an area that, according to government economists, suffered a *$150 billion* loss. The destruction of homes, businesses, roads, bridges, and infrastructure swept away jobs as well; an estimated one million local residents from New Orleans to Mobile were left unemployed indefinitely, and Hancock County suffered a near 100 percent unemployment rate. This not only decimated municipal, county, and state tax coffers, but also the lives of the unemployed.

With the area's ability to generate revenue through sales, tourism, and taxes reduced to near-zero, and facing a monumental cleanup and rebuilding task at hand, many residents simply left. One day, they said, they would be back. One day, they said, they would return to the area their families had called home for as many as nine generations . . . but when?

On the Ground: 2008

You'd never know from the contagious spirit of optimism now evident here that Hancock County residents had suffered through a devastating hurricane less than three years ago. People are again working, talking about their futures, enjoying the company of their friends, going to school, and buying groceries, household goods, and all sorts of retail products. Led by the passionate determination of Waveland Mayor Tommy Longo and Bay St. Louis Mayor Eddie Favre, and supported by enormous investments of time, money, and energy from out-of-state businesses, developers, and builders, Hancock County is becoming a model of recovery from catastrophe.

When Bay St. Louis residents commemorated the two-year anniversary of Katrina on August 29, 2007, they looked around and saw plenty of familiar faces. The situation has only continued to improve. The city's population stands at 98 percent of its pre-Katrina level—an astonishing return rate, considering that, just an hour away, New Orleans is struggling to maintain half its pre-Katrina level population. The Hancock County employment rate is identical to what it was before the storm, reflecting a statewide reclamation of seventy thousand jobs that were lost. The crown jewel of Bay St. Louis' recovery, a sparkling new city hall, rises from an old electric utility complex on the city's primary artery, U.S. Route 90.

The recovery looks just as promising when viewed from under a hard hat. More than thirty thousand building permits have been issued since Katrina, resulting in a rapid rebuilding of the infrastructure and business community. The new Bay St. Louis-Pass Christian Bridge again brings businessmen and women, workers, and tourists into Hancock County. Annual retail sales have increased 61 percent from pre-Katrina levels. Property values have actually increased, foreclosures are running at a small fraction of the epidemic level sweeping the rest of the country, and dozens of municipal projects are underway in both Bay St. Louis and Waveland. In all, according to Mayor Favre, more than $100 million in infrastructure replacement and improvement is scheduled or underway in Bay St. Louis, and another $60 million worth of work is underway in Waveland. Key infrastructure elements— electrical and gas lines, drainage culverts, and more than half of the water and sewer lines—have been returned to service.

Business is booming here during a national economic downturn, almost everyone is back home, and city officials and residents alike are optimistic—what a difference! Now, on the streets, officials and citizens don't talk about whether Hancock County will recover, but about how much bigger and better it will be than it was before Katrina struck. They don't talk about this recovery taking ten or twenty years, as was reported and feared after the storm; they talk about it happening right now, and growing by the day!

First, a Reality Check

But first, a reality check.

Although the population of Hancock County stands at 98 percent of the pre-Katrina level, not everyone lives in the home he or she desires. Many are renting houses or apartments, or staying with relatives. An estimated fifteen thousand people continue to live in FEMA trailers. Many students in the Bay St. Louis-Waveland School District continue to learn in deteriorating portable buildings. The two main cities and the county are under storm-related debt that need to be refinanced or paid off by 2013.

Worst of all for residents, after the initial recovery, the flow of volunteers tapered to a trickle. Residential construction slowed to a crawl, leaving half of Cedar Point and the beachfront still vacant. With FEMA's rent subsidies coming to a close and trailer pick-up imminent, the question looms large: where do the inhabitants go when all they want to do is go home?

One of the Greatest Investments of Our Lifetime

Here is where we, and, I hope, you, come in. The federal government and the Mississippi Development Authority have created a tremendous investment opportunity whereby out-of-state investors can purchase homes, rent them to residents, then implement a strategy that works for their particular financial situation and investment portfolio. Some will sell the home after the five-year period, enabling them to take full advantage of the Small Renter Assistance Program's forgivable loan program, which I recommend (see chapter 9). However, owners may choose to hold on to the house to bolster their real estate portfolios.

Under this program, everyone wins.

The resident leases, or leases to own, an affordable one- to four-bedroom property he or she can call home, with the rental rate tied to average median income, rather than to a landlord's whims. This is a golden opportunity to rebuild a life stymied by Hurricane Katrina; it offers the time to make sure that job, family, and future are in place, plus a chance to secure that new future by buying the house from the investor.

The community benefits from having that resident back home, participating in the local economy that is recovering so well from Katrina that, eventually, it will surpass its highest pre-Katrina levels.

The investor/home buyer receives favorable down payment and financing terms, a forgivable loan potentially equal to 20 to 25 percent of the price of the house, unmatchable tax incentives that include a 50 percent bonus depreciation in the first year, the opportunity to purchase up to twenty homes with these incentives, and the ability to sell the property to the renter or another buyer at any time. For investors who receive State Rental Assistance Program money, it is even more advantageous to hold the property for more than five years, so that the loan becomes fully forgivable.

Best of all, you don't have to be bothered with the daily details of managing the nonresidential property, dealing with the various regulations tied to this program, or even collecting the rent; that's my job, through my local property management company, A-Shore-Bet Property Management, LLC.

The resident and the community get all the spoils of the program, as do you, the investor. Have you ever heard of such a program in which everyone wins, and wins big? You will by investing in the GO Zone. Developers and builders throughout the Gulf Coast are embarking on programs aligned with the federal government's Gulf Opportunity Zone Act of 2005 and their respective state's development and rental assistance programs.

We're right in the middle of this exciting program. It offers the greatest tax incentive of my lifetime and also a way for you to participate in helping the victims of Katrina, something you might have felt helpless to do in the fateful summer of 2005. Furthermore, it offers an opportunity for you to greatly expand your portfolio and asset base at the same time.

CHAPTER

2

What Is the GO Zone?

When President Bush declared the Hurricane Katrina impact zone—the entire states of Louisiana, Mississippi, Florida, and Alabama—a disaster area on September 14, 2005, FEMA created the Gulf Opportunity Zone, also called the Core Disaster Area or GO Zone. In doing so, the federal government set in motion one of the greatest and most incentivized building booms in recent history. All you need to do is fly to Mississippi, Alabama, Louisiana, or parts of western Florida to immerse yourself in the spirit of renewal and optimism that ranks right at the top of any massive building project with which I've ever been associated!

I'm not alone. Perry Nations, the director of workers' compensation and legislative services for the Associated General Contractors of Mississippi, told the *Mississippi Business Journal*, "It is unbelievable. Everyone is getting busy. There is a tremendous amount of private construction going on, with people trying to get the advan-

---

1 Becky Gillette, "Construction Boom in Mississippi," Mississippi Business Journal, Mar. 26, 2007.

tages of the GO Zone. There is more construction available right now than I can ever remember in the past 30 years."[1]

Between the need for buildings, the recent build-build-build economy, and tax incentives connected to GO Zone construction efforts, developers, builders, real estate agents, and investors are reaping their just rewards for bringing residents home and reigniting an entire region.

That private sector does not only consist of the local residents opening their purse strings. It also consists of you and me participating in rebuilding the GO Zone and helping people return home and involved in their local, regional, and state economies. The best news? We're still in the early stages, but the window has timelines. All of the rebuilding revolves around the GO Zone Act of 2005, which was created to encourage the private sector to participate in this unprecedented rebuilding challenge. Congress' swift action and development of the act (bill number HR 4440), which was signed into law by President Bush on December 16, 2005, provided special tax benefits to those who built properties that they placed in service in the GO Zone after the hurricanes and before the end of 2009 (Alabama) or 2010 (Louisiana and Mississippi). With this act, not only can investors become privy to these new and exciting financial advantages, but they can also help strengthen an ailing, yet quickly recovering, region. Most importantly, we're helping displaced locals return to their homeland by investing in properties and giving them the chance to eventually own them.

Where is the GO Zone?

The GO Zone covers most, but not all, areas damaged or destroyed by Hurricanes Katrina, Wilma, and Rita. FEMA originally determined that residents and businesses within the designated areas would be eligible for assistance from the federal government. These areas were also selected because they could benefit most from rebuilding, for which the government created incentives for businesses and private investors. The designated GO Zone territories are listed below.

Hurricane Katrina GO Zone

In Alabama, the Hurricane Katrina GO Zone consists of the following counties: Baldwin, Choctaw, Clarke, Greene, Hale, Marengo, Mobile, Pickens, Sumter, Tuscaloosa, and Washington.

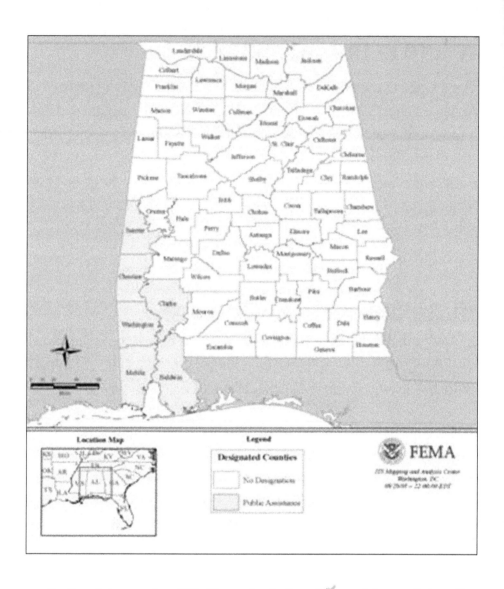

In Louisiana, the GO Zone includes the parishes of Acadia, Ascension, Assumption, Calcasieu, Cameron, East Baton Rouge, East Feliciana, Iberia, Iberville, Jefferson, Jefferson Davis, Lafayette, Lafourche, Livingston, Orleans, Plaquemines, Pointe Coupee, St. Bernard, St. Charles, St. Helena, St. James, St. John the Baptist,

St. Martin, St. Mary, St. Tammany, Tangipahoa, Terrebonne, Vermilion, Washington, West Baton Rouge, and West Feliciana.

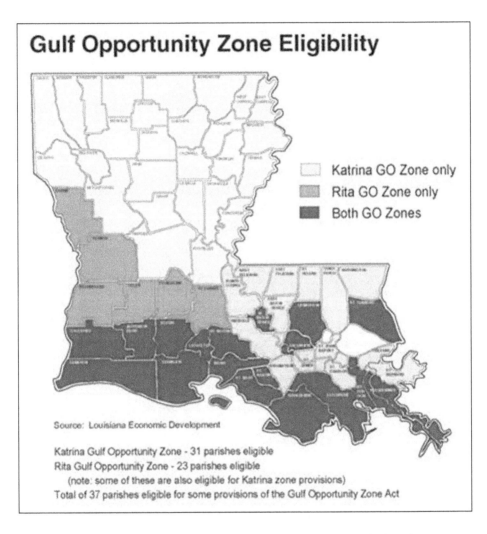

Gulf Opportunity Zone Eligibility

☐ Katrina GO Zone only
▦ Rita GO Zone only
■ Both GO Zones

Source: Louisiana Economic Development

Katrina Gulf Opportunity Zone - 31 parishes eligible
Rita Gulf Opportunity Zone - 23 parishes eligible
  (note: some of these are also eligible for Katrina zone provisions)
Total of 37 parishes eligible for some provisions of the Gulf Opportunity Zone Act

And in Mississippi the GO Zone consists of the following counties: Adams, Amite, Attala, Choctaw, Claiborne, Clarke, Copiah, Covington, Forrest, Franklin, George, Greene, Hancock, Harrison, Hinds, Holmes, Humphreys, Jackson, Jasper, Jefferson, Jefferson

Davis, Jones, Kemper, Lamar, Lauderdale, Lawrence, Leake, Lincoln, Lowndes, Madison, Marion, Neshoba, Newton, Noxubee, Oktibbeha, Pearl River, Perry, Pike, Rankin, Scott, Simpson, Smith, Stone, Walthall, Warren, Wayne, Wilkinson, Winston, and Yazoo.

Hurricane Rita GO Zone

In Louisiana, the Hurricane Rita GO Zone includes the parishes of Acadia, Allen, Ascension, Beauregard, Calcasieu, Cameron, Evangeline, Iberia, Jefferson, Jefferson Davis, Lafayette, Lafourche, Livingston, Plaquemines, Sabine, St. Landry, St. Martin, St. Mary, St. Tammany, Terrebonne, Vermilion, Vernon, and West Baton Rouge. And in Texas, the GO Zone included the following counties: Angelina, Brazoria, Chambers, Fort Bend, Galveston, Hardin, Harris, Jasper, Jefferson, Liberty, Montgomery, Nacogdoches, Newton, Orange, Polk, Sabine, San Augustine, San Jacinto, Shelby, Trinity, Tyler, and Walker.

Hurricane Wilma GO Zone

In Florida, this GO Zone consists of these areas: Brevard, Broward, Collier, Glades, Hendry, Indian River, Lee, Martin, Miami-Dade, Monroe, Okeechobee, Palm Beach, and St. Lucie.

A Wealth of Tax Breaks & Opportunities

When established, the GO Zone provided numerous short-term tax breaks for affected individuals, tax breaks that included the extension of filing deadlines and of tax payments and contributions; it included as well the forgiveness of interest and penalties, qualified hurricane distributions, displacement exemptions, education credits, tax relief for temporary relocation, consideration for casualty and theft losses, extension of carrybacks of property losses from two to four years, and much more.

The establishment of the GO Zone also provided a tremendous investment opportunity for the rebuilding of the Gulf Coast, which is what caught my attention as a real estate executive, investor, and someone who cares deeply about the well-being of others. Within IRS Publication 4492, produced for taxpayers affected by Hurricanes Katrina, Rita, and Wilma, lies a veritable gold mine of breaks, incentives, bond provisions, allowances, credits, and opportunities for businesses and investors interested in the rebuilding of the Gulf Coast. The center of this rebuilding effort identified in my book is the creation of houses that the displaced and relocated residents can return to and own within five years, while the investors, the builders, and so forth experience the financial and emotional benefits of lending themselves to this unique real estate investment opportunity.

IRS Publication 4492 lays out the business and private investment features of the Gulf Opportunity Zone Act of 2005, which we will discuss in greater detail later in this book. Some of those features are as follows:

- Special depreciation allowance: A one-time, 50% depreciation allowance for qualified GO Zone property, without dollar limit, taken for the first year the property is occupied (purchased *after* August 27, 2005, and placed into service by December 31, 2010, in the case of Mississippi and Louisiana residential real property; placed into service by December 31, 2009, in the case of Alabama property);

- Tax break: no property taxes on properties for up to twenty years as they continue to increase in value;

- Work opportunity credits;

- Employee retention credits;

- Housing credits for in-kind lodging of qualified employees;

- Reforestation cost deduction of $10,000;

- Up to 50% deduction for demolition and clean-Up costs;

- Increase in rehabilitation credit from 20 to 26% for structures rehabilitated between August 27, 2005, and January 1, 2009.

A-Shore-Bet Property Management's Place in the GO Zone

Like millions of fellow Americans, I wanted to roll up my sleeves and help the beleaguered citizens of Louisiana, Alabama, and Mississippi as soon as I saw the first televised images of the havoc wrought by Hurricane Katrina. The Gulf Opportunity Zone Act provided a unique combination of tax breaks, incentives, and allowances for me to create investment opportunities for myself and others while helping the people of the affected region rebuild their lives.

That is where A-Shore-Bet Property Management, LLC, comes in. I started A-Shore-Bet to assist investors with managing residential real property in the Mississippi, Alabama, and Louisiana GO Zones. It educates investors on the specific benefits and features of the Gulf Opportunity Zone Act and the GO Zone, locates properties, and assists with the attainment of funding.

In addition, we assist with the placement of investors in two developments overseen by A-Shore-Bet: Shore Acres and Waveland in the Mississippi Gulf Coast community of Bay St. Louis. Bay St. Louis was one of the hardest-hit cities, as it was located in the devastating eastern quadrant of Hurricane Katrina's path. A fifteen-foot tidal surge, combined with twenty-foot seas, 140-mile-per-hour winds, and three days of floods from the rains leveled the community's homes and businesses. There was a near-complete displacement of local citizens and businesses.

That was then. The picture is different now. Bay St. Louis is on the rebound. Citizens are returning home. New houses are rising on the verdant landscape, while those that survived Katrina are being elevated onto platforms that can withstand future tidal surges. Businesses are coming back to town. And we're in the middle of this exciting period of recovery and growth, listening to residents' stories, hearing their dreams for the future, and helping them attain their personal, familial, and business goals. In the process, we're also creating a once-in-a-lifetime investment and tax incentive opportunity throughout Waveland, Bay St. Louis, Biloxi, and other locations we manage.

The remainder of *Investing in the GO Zone* specifies the details of this remarkable opportunity and how qualified investors can take major steps toward expanding their property and financial portfolios. In doing so, we're participating in one of the few bona fide building booms of these times and turning the GO Zone into a true opportunity for the locals who have called the area home for countless generations.

CHAPTER

3

The Government Does Care

The initial television broadcasts of Hurricane Katrina's devastation told a story of suffering and chaos experienced by those at the

center of the tragedy, suffering that was felt at the highest levels of government and throughout the world.

Initially, the federal officials reflected the reaction of America: they gasped like someone who had just received the greatest imaginable shock. The disaster overwhelmed the government's emergency response programs and caught FEMA off guard during the middle of its absorption into the newly formed Department of Homeland Security. It left local, state, and federal leaders scrambling for ways to rescue trapped and stranded citizens, restore civil order, and figure out how to rebuild an entire region that, as a National Guard officer who had served two tours in Iraq said, "was more devastating than anything I ever saw in Iraq, and I was in the fight for Fallujah, and also in Baghdad during some of its worst times."

Like everyone on the ground, the government scrambled to provide an appropriate response. Officials assured residents that they would receive help, as the government tried to put together the most massive domestic relief program in American history. Government agencies, relief organizations, contractors, builders, power companies, and private citizens converged upon the impact zone—a 150-mile region east and west of New Orleans, extending 100 miles north and down to the southernmost parishes—to provide assistance. Some of the efforts were remarkable in their vision. For instance, a magazine publisher from Florida rented three U-Haul trucks, enlisted the help of his brother and three other friends, gathered donated goods from additional friends and colleagues, then spent $50,000 of his own money for supplies. Within two days, the caravan was unloading in a neighborhood in Metairie, Louisiana. In the meantime, the government was already crafting the basis of what would become the Gulf Opportunity Zone Act.

The Federal Government's Rapid Long-Term Response

While everyone from President Bush on down was being maligned for "slow" and "insensitive" response to the disaster, the Congress and the administration worked fast to facilitate the building of a tangible future for the devastated area. They knew the economy had to be rebuilt, along with the buildings. They also knew federal disaster relief dollars were finite, and the appropriated $30 billion would be utilized fast. The coffers hadn't yet recovered from the claims of a destructive 2004 hurricane season and a devastating series of tornadoes in the spring of 2005. Members of Congress moved toward a solution by appropriating far more money and incentives than the government had previously provided for a natural disaster.

And they moved fast. Hurricane Katrina hit the Gulf Coast on August 28, 2005, followed shortly thereafter in late September and October by Hurricanes Rita and Wilma, respectively. All areas were immediately declared federal disaster areas, and relief funds started flowing in. On September 15, 2005, FEMA and the Bush administration established the Gulf Opportunity Zone. Just over three months later, on December 16, Congress passed House Resolution 4440, or the Gulf Opportunity Zone Act. Five days later, President Bush signed the act into law.

Department of the Treasury
Internal Revenue Service

Publication 4492
(January 2006)
Cat. No. 47514V

Information for Taxpayers Affected by Hurricanes Katrina, Rita, and Wilma

Get forms and other information faster and easier by:

Internet • www.irs.gov

Contents

Introduction

This publication explains the major provisions of the Katrina Emergency Tax Relief Act of 2005 and the Gulf Opportunity Zone Act of 2005.

Useful Items

You may want to see:

Publication

❏ 526 Charitable Contributions

❏ 536 Net Operating Losses (NOLs) for Individuals, Estates, and Trusts

❏ 547 Casualties, Disasters, and Thefts

❏ 946 How To Depreciate Property

Form (and Instructions)

❏ 4506 Request for Copy of Tax Return

❏ 4506-T Request for Transcript of Tax Return

❏ 4684 Casualties and Thefts

❏ 5884 Work Opportunity Credit

❏ 5884-A Credits for Employers Affected by Hurricane Katrina, Rita, or Wilma

The Gulf Opportunity Zone Act is a piece of legislation that, for all of its tax breaks, tax incentives, and other benefits, demonstrates that *the government does care*. This legislation truly has a "by the people, for the people" feel to it: one group of people utilizes the provisions of the act to develop businesses and nonresidential real property that another group of people—the citizens living within the GO Zone—occupies and later owns. It enables the government to work around its own hamstrung policies on assisted federal housing, offering a means by which citizens can eventually own the homes that are developed in the GO Zone, rather than doing nothing for their futures in subsistence housing. The Gulf Opportunity Zone Act utilizes taxpayer dollars and the financial acumen of developers, contractors, architects, CEOs, entrepreneurs, and real estate executives to spur investment and rebuilding rather than dumping them into another publicly supported or short-term assistance program that cannot possibly be sustained in the long haul.

Serving the Long Haul

The long haul is what we're talking about here, or, to be more precise, building now to create long-term growth for the area. That's what Congress and the administration understood when they created this act, which they managed to work through during a time when they were assailed for not helping enough. However, this act also offered tremendous short-term tax benefits in 2006 to individuals who had suffered losses of homes, jobs, businesses, family members, friends, and a distinct way of life when the hurricanes roared ashore, Lake Pontchartrain's levee broke, and the landscape of the Gulf Coast changed forever.

The government also understood that financial resources in the GO Zone were, and are, deeply strained at all levels, from local and state governments to businesses and residents. The hurricanes' enormous hit to the economies of Alabama, Mississippi, and Louisiana, which by now totals in the hundreds of billions of dollars, made it impossible for residents and businesses to immediately turn to local or state agencies and programs for help. Insurance companies were besieged by claims, and banks were weakened by foreclosed (destroyed) properties, unpaid mortgages and loans, loss of savings, and loss of capital from their business customers. With businesses destroyed and more than one-third of the population displaced, consumerism as we know it came to a screeching halt. The resulting loss of jobs and residents cost the affected state governments billions in lost tax revenues.

Mississippi Small Rental Assistance Program Application Guidebook

Obtaining Development Money: Mississippi's Program

In addition to the federal response, the governments of the four GO Zone states—Alabama, Mississippi, Louisiana, and Florida—developed differing programs on providing loans to investors interested in building homes. Mississippi has been quite proactive in bringing investment opportunities that help its residents, with the creation, for instance, of the Mississippi Development Authority (MDA) that offers a Small Rental Assistance Program and other means for people to obtain cash for investment within its borders.

The key to Mississippi's program is the Small Rental Assistance Program, which offers a loan of up to $30,000 for each new home to be built. If the project is completed within six months of loan approval, and the owner holds on to the house for five years, another $10,000 bonus kicks in *and* the loan becomes fully forgivable (see chapter 9).

The Small Rental Assistance Program also enables investors to choose one of four program options, each targeted at a different type of rental housing property:

a. Rental income subsidy assistance

b. Repair or reconstruction reimbursement for Katrina-damaged property

c. Repair or reconstruction reimbursement for non-Katrina damaged property

d. New construction reimbursement

For the purposes of investing in nonresidential real property in the GO Zone, we'd normally focus on items b, c, or d. However, the MDA program has made it possible to apply for the rental income subsidy allowance if the amount needed for construction on a unit is less than the maximum loan amount.

The features of the MDA Small Rental Assistance Program are enticing. In Program D, the New Construction Reimbursement, we find the following:

- Up to a $40,000 forgivable loan *per unit*, to be used for construction. The forgivable loan schedule scales from 0% in years 1 and 2 to 33% per annum in years 3 through 5 (See chapter 9).

- A maximum $30,000 payout schedule, 50% of which is to be delivered when the building permit is secured, and the rest upon presentation of a Certificate of Occupancy (COO).

- A loan interest rate set at the London Interbank Offered Rate (LIBOR) plus 1%.

- Investor agrees to rent units to tenants at or below 120% of the Area Median Income (AMI) ($40,000 to $79,800, depending upon the county and the number of people in the household), but that a majority of the rental units in an individual property must be offered at 80 % of AMI ($27,000 to $46,750, depending upon the county and the number of people in household).

Besides the tax and investment values of this program, it also offers what I consider a golden nugget for developers and investors participating in multiple-unit buys: forgivable loans stretched over a five-year period. Investors who meet the program terms for the full five-year period will receive complete forgiveness of the principal, a schedule that begins to draw down in year 3. They will also not be required to pay interest.

I will specify all of the features and requirements of the MDA program in chapters 5 and 6. From this small sketch, it is clear how far Mississippi has gone to ensure that its GO Zone communities are rebuilt, and to make it highly advantageous for outside investors with available monies to handle the rebuilding.

Drawing Out-of-State Investors

The federal government has worked with state governments, such as Mississippi's, to make it enticing for out-of-state investors to participate in the rebuilding of the Gulf Coast. They created a program so beneficial to the investor and helpful to the citizenry, that it is, to quote the title of chapter 6, "the greatest tax incentive of my lifetime." At a time when many thousands folded up their tents and thousands of others thought of doing the same, the government offered a way to rebuild that could make everyone feel good. When I see an opportunity such as the GO Zone Act that offers breaks and incentives and leaves me feeling good to have profited handsomely while helping others to get on their feet, I'm in. And you should be as well.

Most of all, the Gulf Opportunity Zone Act is a great initiative for investors to balance their desire for making money with that of expressing compassion for the plight of the Gulf Coast residents. The government showed its caring by understanding this balance, a reaching out exemplified by one stipulation more than any other: nonresidential real properties that are developed within the tax incentive parameters of the GO Zone Act are offered on a rent-to-own basis to local residents, who can buy their homes within five years.

There's more. If a home is purchased after two, three, or four years, the terms for the final years of the loan made to the investor are prorated and forgivable.

Thus, the investor collects rent, receives major tax breaks and incentives, including a 50 percent first-year depreciation on the value of the property, and he or she can look forward to selling the home to its local occupant within the five-year time frame. In that period of time, the investor will have recouped his dollar-for-dollar outlay, received six-digit tax breaks deducted directly off his or her adjusted income, and earned rental income. Throw in the principal incentive of the Small Renter Assistance Program, which is potentially the full forgiveness on a building loan, and you have succeeded in greatly lowering your tax exposure, with a very small fraction of the value coming originally from your hard dollars.

The final caring gesture of the government is reflected in what I like to call quantum living or investing: an individual entity can own up to five new homes. So, for instance, if you divided yourself into four entities, you could own up to twenty properties. Each property would provide the full set of tax incentives, deductions, and allowances, the highlights of which I shared above, but which I will explain again in full detail in chapters 5 and 6.

See what I mean? It's the best tax incentive of my lifetime and, possibly, yours. It comes to us from a government that responded to an unparalleled natural domestic disaster the only way it could, by realistically appealing to the fiscal and developmental creativity and energy of the people.

With the Gulf Opportunity Zone Act, the federal government has created a true win-win situation for investors as well as residents.

But it is the spirit of those residents that will convert this recovery into a thriving Gulf Coast throughout this century.

Let's meet them.

CHAPTER

4

We the People (Living in the GO Zone)

The GO Zone is rocking. Everywhere you turn, builders are construct-ing new homes, and surveyors and developers are sizing up vacant lots.

Residents are moving out of FEMA trailers or coming back home to find houses, jobs, opportunities, and business structures waiting.

What a difference from the scene Waveland Mayor Tommy Longo described in late October 2005: "[The problem we faced] was having a task and knowing what to do and having the people capable to do it, just not having the resources to do it, whether it be vehicles, or parts, or pipe, material, even sand or clay. My God, we'd have given anything for a golf cart."

Thankfully, that sense of helplessness, when local businesses and residents desperately tried to clean up their devastated homes and towns with little or no resources, is a memory. Yet it demonstrates what this GO Zone building boom and our investments as nonresidential homeowners are all about: providing homes and business structures for a remarkable group of people who began looking forward—rather than wallowing in their tragedy—the day after Katrina leveled their homes and livelihoods.

The same people we saw on TV, wading through millions of cubic yards of debris and standing in piles of rubble that used to be their homes, are fueling the rebuilding effort that is bringing their communities back to life—a potentially better life than before Katrina. They've been joined by an incentivized business and private sector that is bringing new construction, new jobs, and new hope to them. The sounds of saws, nail guns, onsite generators, and conversations in many regional dialects and accents fill the air.

The GO Zone Act and the private sector might be the money behind this tremendous boom, but the local residents are the energetic and spiritual driving force. Without their resilience, hospitality, strength, willingness to work with outside companies and investors, and dogged determination to recover from the definitive disaster of their lives, we would be still be looking at a wasteland dotted with massive piles of debris, tent cities, and FEMA trailers.

"Most everyone I know is in some stage of rebuilding," writes Mississippi resident Heather Harper. "I feel like we are living in some house flipping or design show. It's funny to see this rural area embracing such modern trends. I never thought I'd hear my father use the term 'cut in' when referring to painting. And I never thought he would have anything on his walls besides paneling!" Heather's comments hint at what I've seen during my trips to the GO Zone: people adjusting their lifestyles to bring their communities to a better place than they were before Katrina, Rita, and Wilma hit.

When did this attitude take root? Look at some of these comments by victims of the storms:

Tommy Longo, mayor of Waveland, Mississippi:

"In some ways we're way ahead of the expectations of FEMA and the state. I had told them all early on, 'You all are underestimating us. We're very resilient and very resourceful. And given just a hand, we'll be way ahead of where you think.'"

Debby Plauche, Waveland, Mississippi:

"I love Waveland. If you look past the debris and rubble, it is still one of the most beautiful settings around and can be a better city than before. One day at a time and with God's grace, we will continue to move forward."

Michael Homan, New Orleans:

"I survived Hurricane Katrina, but it transformed me. I am a different person. I feel more loved than I did a week ago. The world clearly has plenty of empathy and compassion left. I saw people slide down ropes out of helicopters to rescue people from rooftops. I saw my neighbors fill up their boats with supplies and row through neighborhoods distributing food and water to those in need. Much of the heroism affected me directly, and touched my heart in a way I will use to return and rebuild."

Dan Marine, furniture dealer, Mississippi:

"A day before the storm I was the biggest used furniture dealer in southern Mississippi. The day after, I was looking for a mattress to sleep on. When it hit, I just kind of shrugged my shoulders and said, 'Oh well, I've got a lot of work to do.' Some people get depressed, and they just can't get out of bed. But you can't allow

circumstances that are out of your control to dictate your life. It just takes perseverance."

Pam West, Bay St. Louis, Mississippi:

"It will get better, and we need all the wonderful help we are getting from everybody all over the country, and one day we will be able to reciprocate. It's a lot harder to accept help than to give it, no?"

Dena Boggan, Florence, Mississippi:

"We Mississippians are a resilient lot. Our entire coast was obliterated, and but for the grace of God and the very brave people in these cities and counties, they would not have survived. Kudos to the quiet dignity our state and local officials have shown."

Kelly Erend, a visiting mother of two teenagers, Catskill Mountains, New York:

"I had the opportunity to visit Biloxi, and the people are awesome. I met the kindest loving people there than anywhere in my life."

These comments were made not in 2006 or 2007 when the rebuilding was underway but shortly after the storm. They strike me as the remarks of brave people who are full of hope and vision at a time when they understandably could have looked to the sky for months or years and asked, "Why me?"

Resourceful, Self-Sufficient People

Deep Southerners are, by nature, resourceful and self-sufficient people. Their reputation as folks who don't care much for outsiders might have some merit, particularly in more insulated, rural regions, but I don't view that as a negative. Rather, I look into their depths and find a can-do spirit and strength that reminds me a lot of the people I see in my Millionaire Challenge Seminars or those I advise on real estate strategies. The people of the Gulf Coast would so much rather give to others than receive assistance, even though many suffered great emotional and financial pain from the storm. In hundreds of thousands of cases, they had to receive assistance, but it did not go over well in their hearts. They vowed to rise and to build even greater homes and communities that would better withstand the next devastating hurricane so that they could get on with their quiet lives where action, rather than words, is the rule.

Now that's the type of person I want my investment to help! It's that can-do spirit that has inspired residents to embrace the local and outside builders and developers and the other changes that have come with the GO Zone Act. They don't want their communities, neighborhoods, and homes to be the same as they were before Katrina, Rita, and Wilma hit. They want them to be better!

One local builder said, "Everywhere just around us, there's a lot of rebuilding going on and construction. We're so excited about helping everyone come back from the storm!" A lifelong Hancock County resident added, "Some people moved away, but I know they want to come back. The growth is good, and I know it's going to get better."

A poignant remark came from a man whose family has been in the region for generations: "A lot of people say they don't want change, they want it to be the way it was before the storm hit . . . well, it ain't gonna be that way. A lot of that way was washed inland with the storm. So let's take this change and make a better life for ourselves with it."

In Their Words: Leaders and Residents Working Together

After spending a lot of time in the GO Zone, I can tell you that the above attitude begins with the community leaders. In one of our core development areas, Hancock County, every bit of dynamic revitalization you see and feel stems from the decisions and actions of five men whose vision I am most proud to share and participate in: Mississippi Governor Haley Barbour, now-retired former Senate Majority Leader Trent Lott, Bay St. Louis Mayor Eddie Favre, Waveland Mayor Tommy Longo, and Hancock County Supervisor Rocky Pullman.

Senator Lott and both mayors, plus their families, suffered personally from the effects of Katrina. All three lost their homes. Mayor

Longo's wife, Theresa, who suffered a broken wrist and cheekbone, spent three days after the storm locating stranded residents, getting supplies to them, and ushering them to safety! Mayor Longo's five children took turns walking many miles along Highway 90, a road dangerously littered with the twisted remains of the prefab metal buildings that used to line the highway. They looked for nearby stores to buy whatever food and supplies they could find, a task the mayor said "was no place for a kid to be. It was no place for anybody to be." This was Mayor Longo's second experience with a devastating hurricane. In 1969, when his father John held the same position, Waveland was seriously damaged by Hurricane Camille.

I particularly loved the way the aforementioned leaders handled the early days after the storm. They set a tone of "action, not words" that now makes southern Mississippi a living testament to successful recovery and rebuilding. Everyone from Governor Barbour on down tried to steer clear of the emotional rhetoric on display in the back and forth between New Orleans, the state of Louisiana, and the federal government. They tried to focus not on words or finger-pointing, but on community meetings, actions, and solutions. Bay St. Louis Mayor Favre quickly set the local tone by staging Saturday morning community meetings in a badly damaged city hall whether or not there was an agenda. Saddened by the loss of his home and the devastation to his beloved Gulf Coast, Senator Lott became the initiator and the driving force behind the GO Zone Act. Governor Barbour quickly followed suit, working with his staff, business owners, and developers large and small to craft what became the Mississippi Development Authority's Small Renter Assistance Program, the other critical peg in the GO Zone development board.

Although Mayor Longo drew some initial criticism for comments he made on the early government response, his later actions proved that those comments were rendered by a man under immense stress that none of us will probably ever experience; he had seen a city destroyed, dozens of residents dead, parts of the city under twenty feet of water, a wife suffering from two broken bones, and five children walking miles to the store to get supplies. The mayor later received compliments from countless residents and business owners for resisting the urge to quick-fix his city. Southerners are known for taking their time to contemplate on decisions, which is often mistaken by others for "being slow." I believe the correct word is *deliberate*, and the mayor's decision to let the waters settle before moving forward was remarkable in both its courage and its correctness.

So what did Mayor Longo do? He welcomed outside developers and builders and their resources. He, his staff, business owners, and citizen leaders thought about how they wanted the new Waveland to look. One of their early acts was to raze and replace those dangerous prefab metal buildings along Highway 90 with hurricane-resistant structures. The mayor convinced Lowe's to establish a new home-improvement retail franchise in town. "The outpouring of support and help from other parts of the country has been tremendous," he said. "Small businesses are coming back, bigger and better than ever. The economy here is getting better. I'm really looking forward to the next few years to see what happens."[2]

Said Waveland resident C. J. Lozano in late 2005, "I agree with the message we have to do it right, not fast. I believe the people who are in a hurry will be the ones who get half-assed work done. We have a great opportunity to start over and rebuild better than before."

President Bush described the perseverance of Mayor Longo during his two-year anniversary visit to Hancock County. "Given what he's been through and given what he has seen, it is remarkable that he's still willing to serve with optimism," the president said. The president's remarks were all the more impressive considering he and Mayor Longo had not seen eye to eye on the government's initial response to Katrina. But, for both men, time bore out the greater measure of what each was trying to do for the hurricane victims and the communities.

Meanwhile, Bay St. Louis Mayor Favre became a national symbol of the area's recovery and rebuilding efforts when he famously donned shorts for 730 straight days, or two years, after the disaster. The storm had destroyed 90 percent of his town; toppled its key eastbound connector, the Bay St. Louis-Pass Christian Bridge;

2 "Waveland Mayor Tommy Longo Says His City Was Cut Off From The World," MSNBC.com, Sept. 1, 2006

reduced its east-west artery, Highway 90, to one or two lanes for months; and ruined its prime source of tourism, the quaint historic district, not to mention the loss of the floating casinos and their huge influx of tax and tourism dollars, or the devastation of the expensive waterfront homes, resorts, and hotels. Yet, the mayor looked ahead immediately. "I really don't think at this point we could do things a whole lot faster," he said. "We've come a long ways." And President Bush noted, "He has dedicated more of his life than he ever dreamed to help rebuild the city he loves."[3]

Business owners in Bay St. Louis agreed. "How far we've come in two years is amazing," insurance broker David Treutel said at the two-year anniversary. Hancock Bank Chairman George Schloegel said, "Once it has taken off, it has moved very, very well."

---

3 Rush Transcript, "Gulf Coast Residents Reflect on Two Years Since Katrina," comments by President George W. Bush, CNN, Aug. 29, 2007

In the report prepared by his office, *Hurricane Katrina Two Years Later*, Governor Barbour noted, "We knew it would take years to recover. The rebuilding and renewal of our Coast after Katrina is a mighty tall order, but our people and the generosity of others are making it possible."

They sure are, and the spirit is contagious. Nothing inspires me more than spirited people with tremendous resolve and energy. Take Mary Perkins of Bay St. Louis, who said to MSNBC after her home was rebuilt seventeen months after Katrina, "I am now totally in my house! Yay! It is definitely a wonderful feeling to no longer have to live in a thirty-by-eight-foot FEMA trailer. I now wonder how I made it in that tin can and did not go stark raving mad. It was a great day when the trailer was hauled off!"

Now that FEMA is hauling off all the trailers, it's time to put these great people into some quality homes and give them a chance to own them. Here is how we will get it done.

5

Creating a Future for Your Family and Theirs: The GO Zone Program

One of the greatest attributes of the Gulf Opportunity Zone Act is its win-win dynamic. The more I speak about the GO Zone at seminars, or take potential investors to onsite tours of the Mississippi Gulf Coast, the more excited I become! The investor, builder, real estate representative, and tenant/buyer all reap the rewards of the program. As investors and real estate agents, we're helping displaced families to return home and reconnect their roots to the Gulf Coast that may well stretch several generations into the past. Meanwhile, we're reaping the benefits of a real estate investment opportunity that, as I've said before, comes along once in a very great while, if that often.

In the next two chapters, I will break down the specifics of the GO Zone program as it affects you, the investor. This program combines and integrates three different policy releases and documents, with which I hope to make you more familiar, and they are the following:

1. The Gulf Opportunity Zone Act 2005, signed by President Bush into law on December 21, 2005;

2. IRS Publication 4492: Information For Taxpayers Affected by Hurricanes Katrina, Rita and Wilma, published by the IRS in January 2006; and

3. The Mississippi Small Rental Assistance Program, updated by the Mississippi Development Authority (MDA) in October 2007

The Gulf Opportunity Zone Act

The Gulf Opportunity Zone Act, or GO Zone Act, was created in a bipartisan effort of the Congress and the White House in the final quarter of 2005, following the disasters of Hurricanes Katrina, Rita, and Wilma. The purpose of the act was to provide immediate short-term tax relief for affected individuals and businesses, and to stimulate rapid future investment in the rebuilding of the most affected areas of Texas, Louisiana, Mississippi, Alabama, and Florida—the GO Zone.

At the signing ceremony for the Gulf Opportunity Zone Act, President Bush encapsulated the short- and long-term benefits to both investors and residents when said, "Today, I'm going to sign the Gulf Opportunity Zone Act of 2005. It's a step forward to fulfill this country's commitment to help rebuild. It's going to help small businesses, is what it's going to do. For small businesses in the affected area, the GO Zone will double expensing for investments and new equipment from $100,000 to $200,000.

"The bill also provides a 50% bonus depreciation, and that means tax relief for small businesses that—and businesses that purchase new equipment and build new structures. In other words, this tax act provides incentives for people to move forward. And as these businesses move forward, they're going to need to employ people. So this is a tax bill that has got employment consequences to it. This is going to help the entrepreneurs of Louisiana and Mississippi and Alabama, entrepreneurship creates opportunity, which creates job.

"This is just part of our plan to help the people get back to work. We've got to help workers get the skills they need. I just met with a group of concerned citizens from business and labor and education, all aspects of society. Again, I want to thank you all for being there. We're talking about how to help put together a strategy that takes advantage of the jobs that are going to be created down there to make sure there's a skill set match. We've got a lot of people that want to work, and yet they may not all be electricians or plumbers. And so one of the real challenges and opportunities we have is to match willing worker with jobs that will actually exist. And that's what we're talking about and strategizing about."[4]

IRS Publication 4492

When released, IRS Publication 4492 focused on three ways to create tax relief, breaks, and incentives for individuals and businesses:

1. Immediate short-term relief in tax years 2005 and 2006 for victims of the hurricanes;

2. Additional long-term tax relief for individuals seeking to rebuild or renovate their damaged or destroyed homes;

3. Additional long-term tax relief for businesses willing to rebuild and reinvest in the area.

---

4 Signing comments of President Bush when he signed the Gulf Opportunity Zone Act of 2005 (House Bill HR 4440) into law on Dec. 21, 2005.

Much of the publication addressed sections with active timelines that have since expired, such as extended tax deadlines, charitable contributions, casualty and theft losses, net operating losses, demolition costs, and more.

It is the latter two sections of IRS Publication 4492—additional long-term tax relief for individuals and businesses—where we find the tax incentives and benefits for investing in the GO Zone. I will break these down in chapter 6.

Mississippi Small Rental Assistance Program

The Mississippi Small Rental Assistance Program is a very proactive effort by the state and its governor, Haley Barbour. At a time when the rest of the nation is dealing with a sluggish housing market, this program will not only bring new housing and development to Mississippi's affected residents, but it will also propel Mississippi's economy to the level beyond what it was before Hurricane Katrina struck. As I like to say, "Location! Location! Location!" Smart investors need to be willing to move their money to where the action is, and the action is in Mississippi!

The Small Rental Assistance Program covers the nuts and bolts of the GO Zone Program in Mississippi, laying down the ground rules for all aspects of the investment and building process, and providing both rules and protections for investors and tenant/buyers once the homes are built.

Qualified GO Zone Property

Both the state and federal GO Zone investment incentive programs pertain to *qualified GO Zone property*. Earlier, I spelled out the respective counties in Texas, Louisiana, Mississippi, Alabama, and Florida that are part of the Gulf Opportunity Zone. Within those counties lie the real properties, developments, and other qualified parcels. According to IRS Publication 4492, qualified GO Zone property within the designated counties includes:

- Tangible property depreciated under the modified accelerated recovery system (MACRS) with a recovery period of 20 years or less.

- Water utility property.

- Computer software readily available for purchase by the general public, subject to a nonexclusive license, and has not been substantially modified. In other words, if someone within the GO Zone lost his or her computer and all software, the new personal and business software would be considered qualified GO Zone property.

- Qualified leasehold improvement property.

- Nonresidential real property and residential rental property. This is the area of primary focus for out-of-state investors.

The following types of property do not qualify, even if they are located within the GO Zone:

- Property required to be depreciated using the alternative depreciation system.

- Property wholly or partially financed with proceeds from a tax-exempt obligation.

- Property for which you are claiming a commercial revitalization deduction.

- Any property used in connection with a private or commercial golf course, country club, tanning facility, massage center, hot tub facility, or any store that primarily sells alcoholic beverages for consumption off premises.

- Any gambling or animal racing facility.

- Property in any class for which you elected not to claim the special GO Zone depreciation allowance.

Purchase of Qualified GO Zone Property

There are a number of time requirements attached to qualified GO Zone property, which include the following:

- You must have purchased the property after August 27, 2005.

- The property must be placed in service by December 31, 2010 in the states of Louisiana and Mississippi, and by December 31, 2009, in the state of Alabama.

- All of the use of the property must be in the GO Zone and in the active conduct of your trade and business in the GO Zone. A real estate property management company, such as A-Shore-Bet, fulfills this requirement on behalf of all the investors whose properties the company manages.

- After August 27, 2005, the original use of the property in the GO Zone must begin with you, the investor. Additional capital expenditures you incurred after August 27, 2005, to recondition or rebuild the property meet the original use test if the original use of the property in the GO Zone began with you. This is fulfilled as well, as the original use of the property post-Katrina is to construct the home in which you invested.

Standard Eligibility and Program Requirements—Mississippi GO Zone

As you consider investing in the GO Zone, there are several standard eligibility and program requirements laid down by the MDA that you should be aware of, and they pertain specifically to the non-residential real property investments with which we're involved.

Eligibility requirements include the following:

- All housing units must be located in official GO Zone counties.

- All properties must contain between one to four units.

- Modular housing is eligible, but manufactured housing is not. We work with Safeway Homes, the number 3 manufacturer of modular homes in the country, and other great companies such as Oak Creek Homes, Modular One, and Palm Harbor Homes. There will be more on this in chapter 7.

- Single-room occupancy properties are not eligible.

- Only units that are unoccupied at the time of application submission are eligible.

- Any applicant, non-profit organization, corporation, or other ownership group may apply for up to 25 reconstruction properties per entity. The maximum total aggregate number of properties for all entities within that group is 100.

- Any applicant, non-profit organization, corporation, or other ownership group may apply for up to 5 new construction projects per entity. The maximum total aggregate number of new construction projects for all entities within that group is 20.

- Applicants may apply for 25 repair/reconstruction properties in addition to 5 new construction projects, for a maximum total of 30. The maximum total combined number for all entities within that group is 120. (Note: A reconstruction project is defined as a partial or complete renovation and/or rebuilding of a home that was severely damaged by Hurricane Katrina.)

- Applicants are prohibited from participating in multiple ownership structures in order to circumvent the maximum number of properties.

- All rental units must meet the following minimum square footage requirements:
  - One-bedroom units: 660 square feet
  - Two-bedroom units: 880 square feet
  - Three-bedroom units: 990 square feet
  - Four-bedroom units: 1,320 square feet

- Owners with felony convictions are not eligible.

Program requirements include:

Liens

- Acceptance of a lien on the rental property in favor of Mississippi Development Authority. The lien is released when your opt-in loan is either forgiven or paid (depending upon when you resell the unit).

Insurance

- Maintenance of casualty (hazard) loss insurance on the structure on the property.

- Maintenance of commercial liability insurance on the rental property.

- Maintenance of flood insurance (if required) up to the maximum amount.

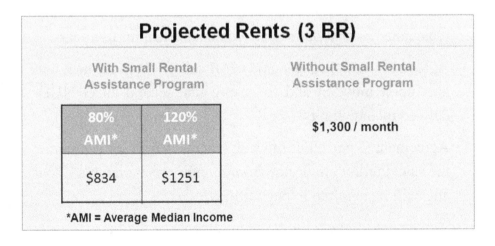

Projected Rents (3 BR)

With Small Rental Assistance Program		Without Small Rental Assistance Program
80% AMI*	**120% AMI***	$1,300 / month
$834	$1251	

*AMI = Average Median Income

Rent Regulations

- Agreement to rent all units to tenants with incomes at 120 percent or less of area median income (AMI), which is set annually by the Department of Housing and Urban Development (HUD). Depending on the area, the maximum allowable rent for a four-bedroom home falls between $1,286.00 and $1,353.00 (see above chart).

- Agreement that 51 percent of the available rental units in each property will be rented to tenants with an income at or below 80 percent of AMI. Depending on the area, the maximum allowable rent for a four-bedroom house is between $857.00 and $902.00.

- For two-unit structures, one unit must be rented to tenants with income at or below 80 percent of AMI, while the other may be rented to a tenant at or below 120 percent of AMI.

- Agreement that sale of the property may trigger repayment of the loan.

- Compliance with HUD affordable housing standards. Rate compliance and property management compliance must be met and maintained as plan-defined affordable housing for five years.

- Agreement to collect income certifications from all new tenants upon move-in and to ensure that tenants meet HUD-defined income limits.

- Agreement to pay all utilities on tenants' behalf, or to subtract the stated utility allowance from monthly rent amounts if tenants will be required to pay utilities.

- Agreement to abide by the requirements of the Fair Housing Act, which prohibits discrimination based on race, color, religion, sex, national origin, familial status, and/or disability.

• Agreement that all tenant leases will solely use the MDA-provided standard lease template, and that the initial lease terms will be for a minimum of six months.

How to Get Started

Now that you've seen the specific MDA requirements for participating in the Small Rental Assistance Program (the enforceable ground rules once you've made the decision to invest and have been approved), let's look at how investing in the GO Zone can work for you.

Let's say you want to invest in the construction of a new home in the GO Zone. For example, the standard sale price for a four-bedroom home is $165,000. You can purchase as an individual or through a business entity that you create, but either way you must work through a licensed real estate property management company located in the GO Zone, such as A-Shore-Bet Property Management, LLC. You will be required to produce a down payment that starts at 10 percent, based on creditworthiness. Ideally, this will be the only hard cash you actually spend in the purchasing process. (Note: In today's environment, given the tightness of credit and the status of the loan, if your credit score is below 700, you will most likely be required to provide a 15 percent down payment. This will depend on the lender and the lender's guidelines.)

Assuming your application is approved by the MDA, you can receive up to a $30,000 loan for a four-bedroom home. All money provided by this loan must be spent to develop the rental property. But there's a great incentive: if the home is made available for tenant occupancy within six months of the original loan closing date, you will receive an additional $10,000 completion bonus. If you own the home for at least five years, the principal and interest on the entire $40,000 will be fully forgiven. I will discuss this further in chapter 9.

Already, you have raised a potential $56,000 toward the purchase of a home, of which only $16,000 came out of your pocket. At the back end, you will receive the 50 percent bonus depreciation for the first tax year the home is occupied. In the case of your $165,000 home, that means you will receive an $80,500 deduction from your adjusted gross income, ensuring yourself a much smaller tax liability. If you have paid $30,000 in taxes over the past five years, you can recover up to $30,000 through the carry-back clause in the GO Zone Act.

Here's what a first-year scenario looks like with a 15 percent down payment:

Purchase Price:	$165,000
Bonus Depreciation:	$ 82,500
Normal Depreciation:	$ 3,003
Tax Bracket:	30%
Potential Tax Savings:	$ 23,849
15% Down Payment:	$ 24,750
Potential Cash Return:	96%

Now, let's say you hold on to the home for five years, and its value appreciates to $265,000, which is a modest number, given the current rate of appreciation in the GO Zone. Here is what happens to your home investment:

Purchase Price:	$165,000
Bonus Depreciation:	$ 82,500
Normal Depreciation:	$ 3,003
Tax Bracket:	30%

Potential Tax Savings:	$ 23,849
Resell Price:	$265,000
Profit:	$100,000
Recaptured Depreciation:	$ 25,000

It's like Uncle Sam giving you a loan at 0 percent interest!

Take the GO Zone Tour

At this point, before you take the big step toward formally investing in a property that, according to MDA requirement, you cannot live in, I would urge you to tour the premises. Many real estate representatives and investment groups do not emphasize physically seeing and touching the ground or nonresidential home you're about to purchase. I do. In my mind, it's simple: if you can afford to purchase a $165,000 home, or a group of homes, then you can afford a few hundred dollars to buy a round-trip ticket to New Orleans or Mobile.

Better yet, take the GO Zone tour we provide through our website, www.thegozoneconnection.com. We will take you to the GO Zone properties we manage, and discuss all the particulars of a GO Zone investment while you are on site. Be sure that you like the location, feel comfortable with its economic growth projections, meet local residents and business owners, and ask questions. We provide this package for $2,495, but like everything else connected with your investment in the GO Zone, it comes with a major incentive: the tour cost is credited directly toward your purchase of a home in the GO Zone!

Getting the Ball Rolling

From this strong start, we will work with you to secure further financing. You can fill out a simple application to begin the loan-approval and escrow process on our website. Once we've processed your application and assigned a lender, you will be preapproved for a mortgage and approved as one of the investors participating in the GO Zone program. Because our property management company, A-Shore-Bet, is licensed and headquartered in the state of Mississippi, we already cover one of the principal concerns of any conscientious out-of-state investor: how do I abide by the residency rules attached to the MDA program?

When the application process is complete and the forgivable loan begins to be released, we obtain a builder to construct the home in which you've invested. We work primarily with Safeway Homes, which is ideally located and has an impeccable reputation that includes, for instance, having complete knowledge and understanding of the building requirements in the GO Zone. I will share Safeway's story more completely in chapter 7.

As soon as your investment home is built and we receive a Certificate of Occupancy from the MDA on your behalf, qualified tenants can then be moved in. They may be returning to the Gulf Coast after having lived out of state since Katrina, or they may be moving into a home of their own after living with relatives, or in FEMA trailers, or in apartments, or other temporary housing. Either way, they are likely to be elated. Another attractive feature of the program is this: if you have relatives in Mississippi that qualify for GO Zone housing, they can occupy the home. Your tenant(s) sign a lease with a minimum six-month term, but the objective of all parties connected with this program is have the tenant(s) eventually buy the home. By law, the home will fall under the management of a real estate property management company such as A-Shore-Bet.

For the next five years, you will pay the mortgage, property taxes, and all the required insurance, while your tenant pays you rent on the AMI-mandated scale. This process will result in a neutral cash-flow status, but that is *absolutely* not where I would suggest placing your focus. Besides receiving the 50 percent bonus depreciation—an $82,500 direct deduction on your adjusted gross income, as noted—you will continue to receive the standard annual depreciation. Your first two years of insurance premiums will be free, compliments of the MDA, plus you'll be sitting on a forgivable loan for which you pay nothing during its term.

Mississippi and Alabama GO Zone Examples

If you purchase a four-bedroom home in qualified GO Zone property in Mississippi or Alabama, you are looking at the following costs and depreciation benefits, based on a 15 percent down payment:

	Mississippi	Alabama
Purchase		
Purchase Price:	$165,000	$200,000
15% down payment:	($24,750)	($30,000)
Gross Loan Amount:	$140,250	$170,000
(Interest Rate: 7.875%)		
Mortgage Calculation		
Principal & Interest:	$1,016.91	$1,232.62
Taxes:	$146.09	$177.08
Insurance:	$166.67	$166.67
Monthly Payment:	$1,329.67	$1,576.37
Cash Flow		
Projected Market Rent:	$1,300	$1,300.00
Monthly Payment:	$1,329.67	$1,576.37
Monthly Negative:	($29.67)	($276.37)
Depreciation Tax Benefits		
Bonus 50% Depreciation:	$82,500	$100,000
Normal Depreciation:	$6,006	$7,280
Total:	$88,506	$107,280

In five years, if not sooner, your tenant(s) will purchase the home from you. You will receive fair market value for it, which, in all likelihood, will translate into a good-sized profit. You can also sell prior to five years if the tenant is ready to buy and you're prepared to release your investment, but you will not receive the maximum benefit of the investment. The forgivable loan will only be partially prorated if it's been in place for three years or more. However, you will still enjoy the federal depreciation benefits.

If I were in your shoes, I would ask the following the questions: Why invest in a property that is tied to various federal and state programs and guidelines? What does it do for me in five years?

Here is a quick five-point answer:

1. You've taken the 50 percent bonus depreciation, plus the standard annual depreciation for each of the other four years. That's a potential adjusted income deduction of more than $100,000 on a house for which you paid $165,000. Under normal regulations covering mortgage depreciation, you'd have to wait eighteen years to accumulate similar depreciation. Looking at it another way, to receive an $82,500 depreciation allowance in a single tax year, such as the one you get through this program, you'd have to buy a piece of property worth more than $2.4 million.

2. You've received a $30,000 MDA loan, earned the $10,000 completion bonus, thanks to your home's rapid construction, and abided by all of its terms. That loan and its interest are fully forgiven. Thus, you've sold the home for $165,000, but your loan exposure was only $109,000 after subtracting the 10 percent down payment and the

---

forgivable loan amount. The $40,000 additional valuation on the house is yours.

3. You've received rental income for five years that substantially offset your mortgage and insurance payments.

4. You're about to resell your home for considerably more than what you paid for it; a valid estimate is a profit of about $100,000 after five years.

5. You've accomplished all of this with a hard-cash investment of just $16,500 (or $24,750, if you paid 15 percent down).

That's how the GO Zone program works. Keep in mind that, in the example I illustrated in this chapter, I spoke of one investor owning one home. You can certainly do that, but the greatest feature of the GO Zone program is that you can—and should, if possible—purchase multiple units. As the Small Renter Assistance Program guidelines make clear, you can purchase up to five different properties as an individual entity, or up to twenty different properties if you buy with multiple entities. Imagine how the benefits would multiply then!

Better yet, let's not imagine at all. I will show you what happens to your federal and state tax picture as an active GO Zone investor.

CHAPTER

6

"The Greatest Tax Incentive of My Lifetime"

As we've toured the Gulf Coast Opportunity Zone and broken down the basic requirements to invest in the GO Zone, I've mentioned that I consider this investment the greatest tax incentive of my lifetime. The Bush administration, the Congressional leaders, and the state government leaders in the five affected states of Louisiana, Mississippi, Alabama, Texas, and Florida knew they needed to create truly special incentives to entice the out-of-state investment interests necessary to renew the Gulf Coast in a timely manner.

In my estimation, measuring their efforts based on my two decades of investment and real estate experience, they outdid themselves by swinging open the opportunity for businesses and real estate interests to rebuild the residential Gulf Coast.

Now, you too can take advantage of that opportunity!

Say someone were to come up to you on the street and say the following:

- I have a program whereby you can carry a huge tax deduction back five years, or carry it forward up to 20 years.

- You can take a first-year depreciation on a $200,000 home, the amount of which would normally be based on a $2.47 million piece of property.

- You can live federal income tax free for the next 20 years.

You'd probably blink or walk away, but not this time, because of these two linchpins of the greatest tax incentive of my lifetime: not only are they government-backed, but they're also written directly into the tax code of the country.

In chapter 5, I summarized the benefits of investing in the GO Zone. Now I'd like to take a closer look at the tax ramifications of your investment.

The Many Gifts of IRS Publication 4492

IRS Publication 4492 (available on our website, www.thego-zoneconnection.com) contains numerous tax incentives, deductions, allowances, and benefits for individuals and small businesses. Many of the tax breaks involves those trying to clean up and restore their lives after the triple whammy of Hurricanes Katrina, Rita, and Wilma in 2005; these short-term breaks have since expired.

Let's summarize what remains. The tax ramifications for those investing in the GO Zone today, who intend to stay with the incentivized program until its expiration date of December 31, 2010, include:

- A one-time, 50% bonus depreciation allowance for the first tax year after a GO Zone property is placed in service.

- Subsequent annualized depreciation at the standard, 3.64% rate for 30-year mortgages.

- A rehabilitation tax credit for pre-1936 buildings and certified historic structures located in the GO Zone. Rehabilitation must be complete by January 1, 2009. The tax credit is increased from 10% to 13% for pre-1936 buildings; and from 20% to 26% for certified historic structures.

- All typical real estate tax deductions remain in force.

The 50 Percent Bonus Depreciation Allowance

The 50 percent bonus depreciation allowance is the huge carrot the federal government has dangled before investors interested in the GO Zone. The beauty of this allowance is that it instantly creates strong incentive to buy and produces a healthy reduction in tax liability. Any time I can say to a client or a group of potential investors, "You're going to buy a $165,000 home and see an $82,500 tax credit for that home in the first year," you can bet smiles fill the room.

There are several provisions and notes regarding the bonus depreciation allowance, which I will spell out below:

- The bonus depreciation allowance pertains only to qualified GO Zone property (see chapter 5). Any other property, even within the affected states and counties, is not covered.

- The bonus depreciation allowance applies only for the first year the property is placed in service.

- The bonus depreciation comes off your adjusted gross income, which will greatly benefit your taxable net income.

- The bonus depreciation allowance is deductible for both the regular tax and alternative minimum tax.

- The bonus depreciation allowance is good for *all* of the properties you purchase. Thus, if you purchase 10 properties in a given tax year at $165,000 per unit, you're looking at a direct tax benefit of $825,000!

- You can elect *not* to deduct the special GO Zone depreciation allowance, but if you make the choice for one property, you must do the same for all property in the same class placed into service during the year.

- Following the use of the bonus depreciation allowance, you will still be eligible to take the 3.64% annual depreciation allowance, which is the standard rate for a 30-year mortgage.

- The deduction can be carried back over the five tax years prior to the time of purchase (2004 through 2008 tax years), or it can carry forward for up to 20 years.

- One caution: if any portion of the property is financed with tax-exempt bonds, that entire property is ineligible for bonus depreciation.

- The use of the bonus depreciation allowance remains subject to normal limitations found in the "at risk" and "passive activity" rules.

Please note that qualified GO Zone homes must be completed and receive Certificates of Occupancy before *December 31, 2010*, in Mississippi and Louisiana, and before *December 31, 2009*, in Alabama to qualify for the bonus depreciation, so time is running short!

How It Works: Individual Unit Investors

Let's say you wish to purchase a single unit in the GO Zone for the standard four-bedroom price of $165,000. For the first tax year after your unit has received a Certificate of Occupancy and your tenants have moved in, you can deduct the entire 50 percent bonus depreciation allowance, reducing your taxable income by $82,500; or you can carry it back for the previous five tax years, reducing your adjusted net taxable income by $16,500 for tax years 2004 through 2008 (if you purchase in 2008); or you can carry it forward for up to twenty years. We recommend you visit with your tax advisor to see whether the one-year lump sum depreciation, five-year roll back, or twenty-year carry forward is best for your tax situation.

In addition, you will receive the standard depreciation allowance for a thirty-year mortgage for the time you own the home. Thus, in addition to the $82,500 bonus depreciation allowance on your $165,000, you will deduct another $3,003 per year off your adjusted gross income. Maintenance and other costs associated with being a nonresidential owner fall under typical homeowner tax deduction guidelines.

Thus, if you simply purchase one home and own it for the entire five-year period of the program, as I discussed in chapter 5, you are looking at the following federal tax benefits from your $165,000 purchase, of which, ideally, only the 10 percent down payment came out of pocket:

- 50% bonus depreciation: $82,500

- Standard annual depreciation: $30,030

- Additional deductible homeowner/maintenance costs: to be determined

What an incredible buy for a homeowner seeking to invest wisely in a nonresidential home for short-term gain!

How It Works: Multiple Unit Investors

If you think the math looks great for the investor who purchases one unit, wait until you see what the federal government has provided for investors who want to take a quantum leap and invest in multiple units. Let's say you want to buy the maximum five properties allowable for a single entity under the GO Zone program. Each property is a four-bedroom unit with a standard $165,000 price tag. Using the tax scenarios and numbers outlined above, here is the exponential result of your choice:

- You are purchasing five units at $165,000 per unit. Your total opt-in cash requirement, assuming good credit and a 10% down payment, is $82,500.

- It's been a great income-producing year, and you need a huge break on the bottom line of your tax return, so you adjust your gross income by pooling up the 50% bonus depreciation allowances you receive for each unit. Your one-year deduction is $412,500, achieved with an initial investment only 20% of that amount!

- You decide to spread out the $412,500 bonus depreciation allowance. You can backtrack it up to five tax years after purchasing the units, or carry it forward for up to 20 years, or any number of combined years between one and 25. If you choose to average it out for all 25 eligible years, you will look forward to an annual deduction of $16,500 from your adjusted gross income. Given your other tax deductions and considerations, and your income, this deduction could put you in a federal income tax–free status for up to 25 years! It's like getting a long-term loan from Uncle Sam for free. Imagine what this will do to free up additional real estate, securities or capital investment dollars, your children's or grandchildren's higher education accounts, or your retirement plan.

The multiple-unit investor creates a huge win-win situation. Not only can the combined bonus depreciation allowance provide annual tax relief at the high five- or six-digit level for up to 25 years, but the investors can literally determine how much bonus depreciation they receive by how many units they purchase.

Here's another scenario for the investor who is able to purchase five units apiece through four entities that have been approved by the Mississippi Development Authority in the qualification process. The investor, in other words, is attached to 20 units. Using the standard four-bedroom price of $165,000 per unit, here is what the numbers look like:

- Total purchase price: $3,300,000

- Total down payment: $330,000

- 50% bonus depreciation, taken in one lump sum: $1,650,000

- 50% bonus depreciation, annualized over 5 years: $330,000 (the same amount as your total down payment)

- 50% bonus depreciation, annualized over 10 years: $165,000

- 50% bonus depreciation, annualized over 25 years: $66,000

- Standard deduction (years 2 through 5), annual deduction: $120,120

Again, these numbers do not include further tax deductions you can anticipate from various homeowner costs. Nor do they include the tremendous opt-in benefit the MDA provides through its forgivable loan program, which ensures that you can invest at the 10 percent down payment rate per unit, depending upon your creditworthiness.

Imagine what you can do with your tax picture now! The GO Zone program's bonus depreciation allowance, coupled with the standard deduction, enables you to reduce your tax liability by up to hundreds of thousands of dollars per year. If you are currently experiencing high revenue/high profit, you could opt to annualize the bonus depreciation for five years.

Or, if you see this as a great way to preserve your nest egg for the long, active retirement you plan to enjoy (or are enjoying), you will certainly accomplish that goal: for the next five years, you'll be receiving an adjustable gross income deduction of $330,000. For the twenty years after that, the deduction would be $66,000 per annum.

There are many ways to work this depreciation allowance into your tax planning, which I would recommend that you explore with your tax advisor.

Ready to check out the homes that you will be purchasing and meet our home manufacturers? Come with me.

CHAPTER

7

Types of Homes

The GO Zone Act is fueling the greatest single building boom the Gulf Coast has ever seen, with hundreds of thousands of new homes replacing destroyed or severely damaged structures from east Texas to the Florida Keys. We're not only in the middle of the action, but on the front lines with the multiple lot developments we sell and manage.

Since September 2007, the state of Mississippi alone has distributed more than $500 million to more than 8,000 homeowners to rebuild homes for tenants under the MDA's Small Rental Assistance Program. Another 2,480 building permits had been issued for new home construction as of early January 2008. On December 22, FEMA jumped back into the act, awarding $400 million to various pilot programs in the GO Zone states to replace its maligned travel trailers with roomier and sturdier housing.

Almost every type and size of home imaginable is being constructed, along with resorts, condominium complexes, casinos, office and industrial parks, businesses of every type, and city and county government buildings. The buildings vary in specification by builder, architect, particular building codes, and whether the developers and builders used tax-free bonds and/or forgivable loans, governed by states and federal regulations pertaining to the GO Zone, to finance construction.

Contractors, developers, and builders are looking at housing structures that include steel, concrete, housing set above stores (as is common in large cities, such as New York City), house-in-a-box kits, log homes, solar homes, duplexes, triplexes, quads, energy-efficient apartments, senior housing, and condos up to twenty stories tall.

For the most part, the buildings have two purposes in common: to get people of all income levels back home and back to work within the GO Zone, and to provide greater safety in the event of another hurricane or severe weather event, which is a common threat along the Gulf Coast.

The primary involvement of A-Shore-Bet Property Management, LLC, with GO Zone investment concerns single-family and multiple-family modular homes. We're not talking about prefab or manufactured homes, nor are we talking about stick-built houses that take many months to build and whose quality can vary greatly from house to house. We're talking about fine three- and four-bedroom single-family and multiple-family modular houses manufactured by two of the finest companies in the business: Safeway Homes of Lexington, Mississippi, and Oak Creek Homes of Dallas, Texas (more on both companies later in this chapter).

Our basic offerings include the following:

Safeway Single Home: Our four-bedroom offering is manufactured by

Safeway Homes of Lexington, Mississippi. Projected sale price as of April 2008: $145,000 to $165,000.

Platinum 8051 Modular Home: Our other four-bedroom offering is manufactured by Oak Creek Homes. Projected sale price: $145,000 to $165,000.

Adroit Towne Homes: Our latest offering, manufactured by Safeway Homes, this multifamily development offers the same features as our single-family homes. Approximate sale price: $325,000 (to be determined upon release).

Because we're making thousands of lots available for development in Mississippi's Hancock, Pearl River, Harrison, and Jackson counties alone, we have recruited the best and the most efficient and expedient companies available. As one of the incentives for an investor to purchase a nonresidential home through the GO Zone Act is the Mississippi Development Authority's forgivable loan, which carries a bonus of up to $10,000 for a four-bedroom home if it is completed within six months of final loan approval, we needed to find builders and companies who would work fast. We had to also take into consideration the needs of the residents trying to get back home or move out of the FEMA trailers in which they'd been living for more than two years! Says Fred Carl Jr., the Hurricane Katrina

Housing Coordinator for Mississippi Governor Haley Barbour, "We need nine or ten thousand homes a year."[5]

We work with four of the companies that are active in the area and making things happen: Safeway Homes, Oak Creek Homes, Modular One, and Palm Harbor Homes. Let's take an inside look at how one of these companies, Safeway Homes, produces the homes in which you would be investing.

The Story of Safeway Homes

When we met Safeway Homes Sales Director Bobby Ingram and learned more about the company, we knew we'd found a partner in our quest to get people home and to offer investors the best house for their dollar. Says cofounder and owner, Buddy Jenkins, of the company he founded with his late brother, Terry, in 2005, "We're really a stick-built house moved in component parts."

Safeway Homes entered the GO Zone market with two major advantages: the company is located in one of the GO Zone states, and the owners are lifelong builders. They know how to make quality houses, and it shows with every Safeway home, which meets standards and requirements far more stringent than those required by the state or any of the GO Zone regulations. "We have three patents on the homes that distinguish them from other modulars," Bobby Ingram says. "We're not mobile homes, we're not manufactured homes. These are built as the owners want them, on site. They're the only modular homes that don't have to go on a slab."

---

5 Becky Gillette, "Construction Boom in Mississippi," *Mississippi Business Journal*, Mar. 26, 2007.

Safeway Homes provide features in both their single-family and multiple-family units (presented and offered by us as Adroit Towne Homes) that other modular home builders and many stick-built home builders simply don't include. These features include total energy efficiency, TechShield attic barriers, pre-engineered structural floor systems, a unique water cutoff feature, hard metal heat and air ducts, prewiring throughout the entire house, and rated wind safety to 160 miles per hour. By comparison, Category 5 hurricane force winds start at 155 miles per hour. In anybody's book, that is a very safe and structurally sound house!

Safeway prides itself on its service performance, which, I can tell you from my experience, is superb. The builders with which Safeway and we work are independently owned businesses with good reputation and solid bottom lines. Safeway offers one other feature that should provide a very nice comfort zone for any prospective home buyer; the builder is responsible for general service to the home for one year after closing! You're not going to find that kind of service from any stick-home contractor.

As of January 2008, Safeway had placed three hundred homes across the Mississippi Gulf Coast, which is three-quarters of all new modular housing since Katrina, and a total of five hundred in the entire GO Zone. Besides our A-Shore-Bet Property Management, LLC, and the Tonja Demoff Foundation, they have also partnered with nonprofit organizations such as Enterprise Corporation, Delta, Habitat for Humanity, and HomeAgain, which is skippered by famed novelist John Grisham, a Gulf Coast resident.

Expect Safeway Homes to become familiar to many thousands more in the coming years, including the investors and tenants we are attracting to the GO Zone through this unique investment opportunity.

The Story of Oak Creek Homes

Oak Creek Homes is our second supplier of modular homes. It is a regional vertically integrated factory homebuilder, with operations in manufacturing, retailing, development, financing, and insurance. Oak Creek, with its two North Texas factories, has been in continuous production since 1983, building more than thirty-six thousand homes. Oak Creek has earned a reputation that is recognized throughout Texas, New Mexico, Colorado, Oklahoma, Louisiana, and Mississippi. It provides a complete line of homes with special custom features, such as adjustable floor plans, to match every lifestyle.

Oak Creek offers its homes through a network of company-owned and independently owned model home centers and builders throughout the southwestern United States. In the past year, Oak Creek deepened its commitment to serve builders along the Gulf Coast, particularly within the GO Zone. In addition to home manufacturing, the company provides financial services to manufactured and modular homeowners. These services include construction, permanent financing, and insurance.

What Is a Modular Home?

Modular homes are often confused with manufactured homes, a common dwelling in the South and other rural areas. I will spell out the differences, though, truthfully, the only thing they have in common is, in some cases, the same manufacturer.

A modular home is a full-sized family house built from quality wood to the highest specifications. Modular homes range in size from simple cottages to small mansions, costing between $60,000 and $500,000 on the market; we work primarily with three- and four-bedroom units with three different floor plans. We also work within the GO Zone cost parameters for three- and four-bedroom homes that range between $165,000 (Mississippi) and $200,000 (Alabama), though we step outside those parameters to offer more exclusive homes to more affluent buyers.

The difference between the construction of a modular home and a stick-built onsite dwelling is that the modular home is assembled at the manufacturer's factory, then trucked to the site, where the components are fused together with the strongest glue and nails on the market. Once they are delivered, modular homes can be completed in days. Furthermore, Safeway Homes is capable of building three homes per day at its Lexington factory. Prior to the implementation of the GO Zone Act, modular homes were primarily built in northern states, which are always challenged by short building seasons and high labor costs.

Conversely, a manufactured home is made of prefabricated metal that is vulnerable to any winds exceeding sixty miles per hour. Manufactured homes also tend to break down and fall into disrepair quickly in hot, humid climates, making them particularly inefficient in the Deep South. The state of Mississippi is so opposed to rebuilding their Gulf Coast with manufactured homes that they have been excluded from any benefits pertaining to the Small Rental Assistance Program.

"It Is the Only Answer"

In a rebuilding situation, such as the one in the GO Zone, modular homes offer tremendous advantages over their stick-built counterparts:

- They're quick to build. (There will be more on the construction process in chapter 10.) We can deliver a Certificate of Occupancy within four weeks of the order, compared with a nine-month average for stick-built homes. Given the necessity to move fast to take full advantage of the tax and investment incentives of the GO Zone Act, including that $10,000 bonus to the forgivable loan I mentioned earlier, this is crucial.

- Modular homes perch easily on stilts to comply with flood zone rules.

- They require less local labor to erect, which is important in any area experiencing a building boom where help can be hard to find.

- Thanks to an October 2006 decision by Governor Haley Barbour and the Mississippi State Legislature, the state's tax on modular homes was reduced from 7% to 3%—saving homeowners between $4,000 and $6,000 per year. No such reduction was given for stick-built or other types of homes.

- Finally, you simply get more home for the money, which keeps the purchase price low enough to make it an enticing investment, especially for those planning to buy multiple units. Says Fred Carl, "It is the answer; it is simply the only answer in Mississippi."

Although you might have to sacrifice a few custom nooks, crannies, or room designs because of the standardized floor plans, you do not lose anything in quality. Rather, you gain a home that goes up quickly, lasts for decades, looks great, creates a great investment opportunity for you, and can withstand one of the greatest of meteo-rological threats: a 160 mile-per-hour Category 5 hurricane wind.

In 2007, about 400 completed modular homes were installed in Mississippi, where the center of our development efforts lay. You can bet that number will increase dramatically in the next three years as more investors participate in the GO Zone. In fact, some experts believe the current interest in modular housing is just a trickle in what will become a flood of new requests. "Really, if we look back 20 years from now, we could see a dramatic shift in the way houses get built," David W. Hinson, professor of architecture at Auburn University, told *The New York Times.*[6]

---

6 Excerpt from Safeway Homes video, provided on Safeway Homes website

CHAPTER

8

Finding a Realtor You Can Trust

Now that you've learned about the GO Zone and clearly see its benefits to your real estate portfolio and tax picture, besides feeling good about helping the Gulf Coast residents who are trying to come home, let's say you've decided to step up and invest. The next and probably the most critical step will be to find a realtor you can trust.

Naturally, with the enticing real estate picture in the GO Zone, numerous realtors have swung open their doors to customers. Nothing can draw a crowd faster than an opportunity developing while much of the housing market works through the current subprime correction. It's safe to say that investing in the GO Zone is the hottest collective real estate opportunity in the nation right now, and you're going to want to buy into it before it's too late.

To do that, it is vital that you work with the right realtor. What does that mean as you look into the GO Zone? What additional qualities should you be seeking in your GO Zone realtor, versus a realtor with whom you'd work to buy a home, office, condo, or other development property in another part of the country?

Feet on the Ground

Your realtor must possess sufficient knowledge of the area to offer you comparisons between your prospective home investment and other homes, communities, and developments in the region. There is only one way to acquire that kind of knowledge: by spending considerable time on location, getting to know the real estate market, the people, the business community, and the short- and long-term economic picture. Provisions in the MDA's Small Rental Assistance Program stipulate that realtors who represent buyers must have a shingle hanging in the state of Mississippi. Our property management company, A-Shore-Bet, is located in Bay St. Louis, right in the heart of Mississippi's Hurricane Katrina rebuilding effort.

If your realtor happens to represent the builders, he or she cannot represent you. In that case, your realtor should act as a consultant for a walk-through, so that you can make sure the developer is performing due diligence when constructing your home.

I have spent considerable time onsite, have picked the very best builders for your home to create tremendous investment opportunities for you, and have firmly established myself as an advocate to all of my clients in the short and long term.

Bring You to the Property

Second, your realtor should vigorously encourage you to touch and feel the property on which the home will sit. Many realtors operate successfully on a sight-unseen premise, which is a practice in the industry, though one I've never followed or endorsed. However, for two reasons, I would definitely steer away from any realtor that tries to sell you a home in the GO Zone without you touring the premises: chances are you've never looked at the GO Zone as an investment opportunity before; and you need to physically see the site of a home to know what you're buying.

We provide a golden opportunity for you to tour the GO Zone, particularly the developments we oversee and manage. Through A-Shore-Bet, we organize monthly tours of the Mississippi GO Zone, when we tour the areas hardest hit by Katrina, show the extensive rebuilding in progress, talk with local officials and businessmen, and give you a chance to visit and choose the lot on which your investment home will be built. Your cost (or investment) for this tour is $2,495, which will be applied toward your down payment and costs for buying a home. You can find out more details and the schedule of trips by visiting our website, www.thegozoneconnection.com.

Expert Knowledge of Programs

Your realtor must be well-versed in both the financing and tax benefit features of the GO Zone Act and the MDA's Small Rental Assistance Program. These features include everything I've discussed in the previous chapters: a diverse combination of tax incentives, depreciation bonuses, forgivable loans, down payment options, rent controls, and more. These monetary matters are different from those that you'll find in real estate transactions in other parts of the country; they're specifically created to renew a devastated part of the country and the people who live there.

Real Estate Investment Strategist, not Just an Agent

I believe your GO Zone realtor needs to be a real estate investment strategist, as well as an agent. Why? Because your decision to invest in the GO Zone involves a cash-neutral position for the short term that weighs its greater benefits in tax incentives and breaks, multiple purchases, and unusual loan structures (the $40,000 forgivable loan, for example), not to mention selling the home at market value, which is certain to appreciate significantly as the GO Zone recovers. You and your accountant will need to decide if your investment should be part of your everyday portfolio, work through your retirement plan, or set up your children's education fund. Although this is part and parcel of any multiple-property owner's planning, investing in the GO Zone involves such extensive immediate incentives, such as the 50 percent bonus depreciation in the first year, that you need a realtor creative and resourceful enough to see how this can work for you strategically while you're negotiating the purchase.

On the financing side (which I've mentioned earlier and will discuss further in chapter 9), your realtor needs to creatively combine traditional financing options with the features available for GO Zone investors, features such as Mississippi's forgivable loan program. Given the times we're in, I would recommend going a step further: your realtor needs to work only with the most esteemed and reputable lenders, especially when bringing you into a home investment tied to both federal and state mandates.

Simplify the Process

Your GO Zone realtor also needs to streamline and simplify the process for you. First and foremost, the GO Zone Act and the Mississippi Small Rental Assistance Program (and other state programs in Alabama, Louisiana, Florida, and Texas) are specific short-term incentives that have been created so private investors can profitably participate in the rebuilding of the Gulf Coast region. In all likelihood, you don't have time to research the minutiae of these programs or the various steps involved in the funding and approval process. Nor, up to now, has the entire process been packaged in a single, easy-to-follow presentation; this book is the first to bring the complete picture to you. Thus, your realtor needs to boil all the information down for you, so you can make an expedient decision, while also providing you solid advice and expertise and answering any of your questions, no matter how general or specific.

Understanding of Available Housing

Many types of homes are being built, and will continue to be built, in the GO Zone in this boom period that is expected to last at least the next twenty years! However, nonresidential home investing requires specific affordable housing to be developed, in the interest of safety and security to owner, tenant, and state. Realtors need to understand the differences between traditional stick-built homes and other housing that is part of the process in the GO Zone—the most notable being modular housing, as far as I'm concerned. Not only do we fully understand the features of modular housing, but we partner with two of the best builders in that business: Safeway

Homes and Oak Creek Homes. This enables us to not only provide investors with knowledge of these homes, but to also guarantee their high quality, numerous features, and safety.

Manage as Well as Sell

If you take advantage of the opportunities afforded by any state development program, such as Mississippi's Small Rental Assistance Program, then your GO Zone investment *must fall under a property management company* that manages your purchase and all that comes with it. It is required that nonresidential homes in the GO Zone program be managed locally. Our property management company, A-Shore-Bet, can represent and manage purchases throughout the five-state GO Zone region, but we feature thousands of lots on two developments that we directly control near Bay St. Louis and Waveland.

The Bottom Line: Full Service

The bottom line is that your GO Zone realtor must be capable of providing full service well beyond the norm. To provide you with the greatest comfort and the maximum bang for your investment dollar, your realtor should be your "go to" person on every issue that is connected with your purchase, from building specs to financial strategizing in your liquid portfolio or retirement plan. You don't have the time or, most likely, the detailed knowledge needed to navigate the GO Zone requirements. You're certainly not going to be inclined to invest in something that may require regular contact with a real estate agent, accountant, financial advisor, contractor, attorney, and property management company just to keep you informed. I can cover all of this ground with my clients as their expert resource to investing in the GO Zone; I believe nothing less will suffice.

Investing through A-Shore-Bet Property Management

We have taken this full-service approach to make your GO Zone investment as simple and seamless as possible. With A-Shore-Bet, you have the comfort and luxury of knowing your investment home will be managed by a team of experts that are local Gulf Coast residents, with Tonja Demoff Companies overseeing the operation. Because this is such a tremendous investment, with a limited window of opportunity—Alabama's window closes on December 31, 2009, Louisiana's and Mississippi's on December 31, 2010—I am personally involved to the extent that I meet with all of the players, set up the buying programs, conduct GO Zone investment seminars, and lead GO Zone tours. What I bring to the table, in addition to a strong property management position in the GO Zone, is my reputation as a tireless worker, a bestselling real estate investment strategy author, and the number two ReMax real estate agent in the country!

As mentioned, we can represent investors looking to buy a property and build anywhere in the GO Zone. We oversee two major developments in Hancock County, which suffered a direct hit and near-complete devastation by Hurricane Katrina. When you invest in those developments, you will be purchasing modular homes at fixed prices, which I elaborated upon in chapter 7.

We work with three types of real estate investors: the individual-property investor, who is looking to buy one or maybe two homes; the multiple-properties investor, who is seeking to buy up to the maximum allowable five homes; and the multiple-entity investor, who can spread his or her purchases across up to four approved business entities, thus potentially owning twenty homes. We have specific financing packages for each.

How to Invest in the GO Zone: A Simple Process

Should you choose to work with us, and we certainly hope you do, we will walk you through a simple process to ownership. The steps from initial consultation to closing are essentially the same as those involved in a typical home-buying transaction; I break them down in the chart that will close this chapter.

We make your initial process simpler and more immediate with our automated transaction process, which you can utilize at any time by going to our website, www.thegozoneconnection.com. You can even invest while you are in the middle of the GO Zone tour. Simply complete the agreement online, after which we will prequalify you and open escrow online. Then our GO Zone specialists will work with you and everyone involved in the transaction process to assure you of a quick and successful transaction.

Let's get to work!

The Home Buying Process

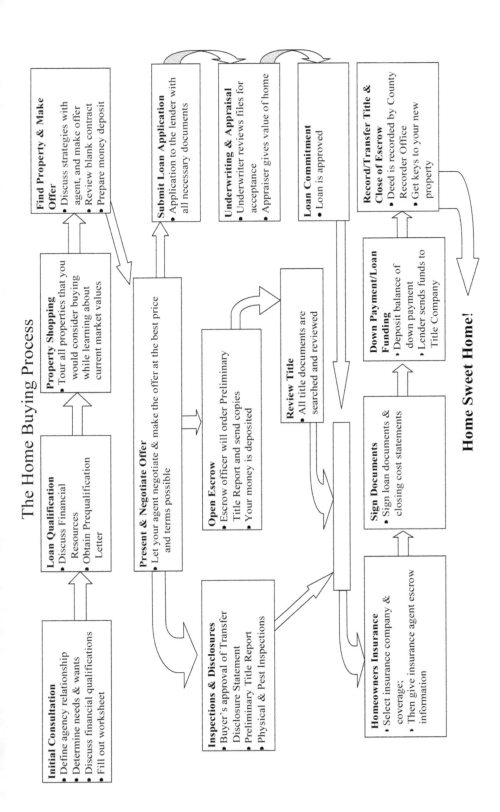

Initial Consultation
- Define agency relationship
- Determine needs & wants
- Discuss financial qualifications
- Fill out worksheet

Loan Qualification
- Discuss Financial Resources
- Obtain Prequalification Letter

Property Shopping
- Tour all properties that you would consider buying while learning about current market values

Find Property & Make Offer
- Discuss strategies with agent, and make offer
- Review blank contract
- Prepare money deposit

Submit Loan Application
- Application to the lender with all necessary documents

Underwriting & Appraisal
- Underwriter reviews files for acceptance
- Appraiser gives value of home

Loan Commitment
- Loan is approved

Record/Transfer Title & Close of Escrow
- Deed is recorded by County Recorder Office
- Get keys to your new property

Present & Negotiate Offer
- Let your agent negotiate & make the offer at the best price and terms possible

Open Escrow
- Escrow officer will order Preliminary Title Report and send copies
- Your money is deposited

Review Title
- All title documents are searched and reviewed

Down Payment/Loan Funding
- Deposit balance of down payment
- Lender sends funds to Title Company

Inspections & Disclosures
- Buyer's approval of Transfer Disclosure Statement
- Preliminary Title Report
- Physical & Pest Inspections

Sign Documents
- Sign loan documents & closing cost statements

Homeowners Insurance
- Select insurance company & coverage;
- Then give insurance agent escrow information

Home Sweet Home!

CHAPTER

9

Getting Financed in the GO Zone

When I first got acquainted with the GO Zone Act and state programs such as Mississippi's Small Rental Assistance Program, I realized that the 50 percent bonus tax depreciation was not the only big benefit. It quickly occurred to me that the Gulf Coast states, Mississippi in this case, were going to lure outside investors with low-interest loan packages. So I looked more closely at the loan program. Its feature was the second golden nugget of GO Zone investing: the forgivable loan.

As a result, getting financed for your GO Zone home investment is not only remarkably easy, but it is also yet another way to stretch your investment commitment without utilizing hard dollars. Whether you're buying one house through your small business entity or a block of twenty-five homes for your LLC or retirement plan, the Gulf Coast states are making it possible for you to possess equity in your investment homes when the Certificate of Occupancy is issued, before your tenant even moves in!

Remember when I said this was the best tax incentive of my lifetime? Well, it's also one of the most appealing investments I've yet seen in terms of financing. If you're qualified and eager to get rolling on your purchase of a home or homes in the GO Zone, we can get you started with or without a down payment check.

Let's take a look at the financing options available to you as a prospective GO Zone homeowner.

Initial Financing—Down Payment

We will finance the down payment of highly qualified investors with credit scores of 700 or above, at a fixed annual interest rate of 7.5 percent as a nonowner occupied stated income loan. Our financing term depends upon several factors, including creditworthiness, amount of money that is financed, and the overall structure of the home purchase deal. On average, our loans are for five-year terms. Monthly payments would break down as follows, based on your purchase of our single-unit $165,000 homes:

10 Percent Down Payment Financing

Homes	Price	Down Payment	Monthly Payment*
1	$165,000	$16,500	$ 352.63
5	$825,000	$82,500	$1,763.13

15 Percent Down Payment Financing

Homes	Price	Down Payment	Monthly Payment*
1	$165,000	$24,750	$ 528.94
5	$825,000	$123,750	$2,644.70

*Principal+Interest+Taxes+Insurance (PITI); the monthly payment figures are approximations.

You can apply for down payment financing when you fill out an initial application to purchase your GO Zone home. You can do all of this—and even pay your down payment, if you do not wish to finance it—through our official GO Zone website, www.thego-zoneconnection.com.

Also, if you embarked on a GO Zone tour with us, the $2,495 fee is credited directly to your down payment and costs associated with buying a property!

Lender Financing

We work only with the strongest and the most secure mortgage brokers/lenders in the business. Thus, when we initiate your escrow process, we will prequalify you, credit your down payment, work with you to qualify for the Mississippi Small Rental Assistance Program's (SRAP) forgivable loan (see below), and secure a preferred lender for the remainder of your balance. This is the one aspect of the financing process that parallels everyday real estate transactions.

Small Rental Assistance Program: Overview

Phase I of the SRAP Homeowner Assistance Program opened in early 2007. This phase, which focused on new building and reconstruction of homes located within the coastal flood plain, closed to applicants on October 26, 2007, after awarding $250 million in aggregate homeowner loans to the four floodplain counties: Hancock, Harrison, Jackson, and Pearl.

Phase II of the Homeowner Assistance Program, which folds in the SRAP, also opened in 2007. Phase II differs from Phase I in that homeowners building outside the coastal flood plain are eligible.

The Phase II verification process is now underway. As of March 10, 2008, a total of 8,176 applications had been received, half of them rollovers from Phase I that had been initially rejected for any number of reasons, creditworthiness not among them. A total of nearly $250 million had been awarded to nearly 3,500 payees, with another 1,250 approved applicants awaiting their initial disbursements. You can track the weekly progress of Phase II by going to www.mississippi.gov. Both of these phases feature a very valuable tool for spurring new construction, the forgivable loan.

How the Forgivable Loan Works

For those who invest in the properties we manage in Mississippi, the key feature of your GO Zone financing package will be the SRAP forgivable loan. This is a remarkable incentive that provides you with up to $40,000 on a four-bedroom, $165,000 home; this is not only an interest-free loan, but also a potentially 100 percent forgivable loan if you meet the guidelines, which I explain below. For those who are building more exclusive, upscale homes, you could be eligible for as much as $100,000!

So, assuming you paid and did not finance your down payment of $16,500, you're looking at an equity of $56,500 before your tenant walks in the door. If you did finance the down payment with us at the Tonja Demoff Foundation, you're still looking at $40,000 in equity upon attaining your Certificate of Occupancy, which means that you have disbursed zero hard dollars for 25 percent of the equity! It only gets better when you purchase multiple homes.

Here's how the forgivable loan works. Assuming you've paid the $50 application fee and your application package has been approved by the MDA, you can receive up to a $30,000 interest-free, forgivable loan for the modular home we will build for you through our manufacturing partners and affiliated builders. All money provided by this loan must be spent to develop the rental property; you may not use any of it to pay the mortgage or for other properties your entity controls. It is strictly a new construction or rebuilding loan.

The loan money will be advanced for new construction in the following manner (based on a $30,000 disbursement):

- Upon attainment of construction Permit: $15,000

- Upon attainment of Certificate of Occupancy: $15,000

Completion Bonus

Once your application and appropriate papers (see below) are reviewed, and the title work is complete, you will have up to two years to utilize the funds for new construction. If it takes longer than two years, you will be considered in default. The completion of the time period is defined as the moment a Certificate of Occupancy is issued for your home to when you receive the final 50 percent of the original loan.

However, if you invest through us, you will not be looking at a ponderous two-year building process. It will be more on the order of one month, thereby setting you up for the bonus incentive that could turn this $30,000 forgivable loan into a $40,000 package.

How? If your home is made available for tenant occupancy within six months of the original loan closing date, you will receive an additional $10,000 completion bonus! That bonus decreases gradually for the next six months, and is eliminated if you cannot complete within a year. Below is a picture of how the numbers break down.

The completion bonus addendum to the MDA's forgivable loan program awards builders and owners that complete a unit within twelve months of original loan closing date the following amounts:

Time	1BR	2BR	3BR	4BR
Original Loan	$22,500	$25,000	$27,500	$30,000
Bonus: 6 Months	$7,000	$8,000	$9,000	$10,000
Bonus: 9 Months	$4,700	$5,300	$6,000	$6,700
Bonus: 12 Months	$2,300	$2,700	$3,000	$3,700
Over 12 Months	0	0	0	0
Total Forgivable Loan + Bonus	$22,500–$29,500	$25,000–$33,000	$27,500–$36,500	$30,000–$40,000

Again, there is no bonus if the Certificate of Occupancy is issued more than twelve months after the original loan-closing date. But that will not be an issue if you work with the Tonja Demoff Foundation and A-Shore-Bet. We want you to receive that bonus. Our primary manufacturing partner, Safeway Homes, can manufacture your home at their Livingston, Mississippi, factory and truck it to the site, where our affiliated builders will set it on its foundation and complete the construction. Your tenant can open the doors to your new modular homes as quickly as four weeks after your loan is approved!

Specific Terms of Forgivable Loan

As mentioned, the loan is an interest-free forgivable loan. The loan principal will be forgiven in equal one-third amounts after the third, fourth, and fifth years of the rental term, as determined by the date the Certificate of Occupancy is issued for the last unit on your property. In addition, the completion bonus will also be forgiven on the same schedule. Should you resell the property prior to the five-year maturity of the loan, you will be responsible for paying back the outstanding principal at 3.5 percent interest. If you opt out or resell prior to the third year, you will be responsible for paying back 100 percent of the loan amount. That figure drops to 67 percent after year 3, 33 percent after year 4, and 0 percent after year 5.

Forgivable Loan Rules and Regulations

There are a number of rules and regulations to remember when utilizing the SRAP loan; they are as follows:

- You can submit an application for the SRAP loan prior to buying the property, but you must provide documentation to show proof of option to purchase. A warranty deed confirming your ownership must be presented at the time of conditional loan closing.

- Once you receive a letter of commitment from the MDA concerning the loan, you will have 60 days to complete the conditional close.

- The loan must be used *exclusively* for construction and/or repair of the home to which it is attached. You cannot use it to make mortgage payments, improvements to other homes, nor shuffle it toward construction costs for other homes you might have purchased in the GO Zone.

- Acceptance of a lien and covenants on the property in favor of the MDA.

- If the lending bank has not yet recorded a deed of trust, the loan will be subordinated to your existing bank loan. If a deed of trust has been recorded, there will be no requirement to subordinate the SRAP loan.

- You can transfer the property to your LLC after receiving the loan without default, provided the LLC was the owner on record at the time of the application, and there is no transfer of control involved.

- You must make the home available to tenants with an option to buy within the loan's five-year period. You must abide by the Area Median Income (AMI) fixed-rent regulations when assigning the monthly rent amount (see chapter 5, page xx).

- The tenant must occupy the home within 90 days of your receipt of the Certificate of Occupancy.

- After the loan term expires, and the entire amount of the loan principal is forgiven, the MDA will release the lien and covenants on the rental property, and you will no longer be bound by the SRAP terms.

- You can apply for up to 30 properties per entity, i.e., five new construction projects, and reconstruction or repairs to 25 existing properties.

- If you default on the loan, the remaining principal balance will retroactively accrue interest from the date of the last loan advance, and all unpaid principal, accrued interest, and termination fees will be due and payable in full on demand.

- If a tenant vacates, you must rerent the property within 90 days.

- You must abide by all construction, residency, tenant occupancy, and other mandates set forth by the GO Zone Act and the Small Rental Assistance Program. I reviewed those earlier in chapter 5.

- Convicted felons are not eligible for this program.

- A fine point: You may also submit an application for the forgivable loan after receiving a Certificate of Occupancy for the now-completed home! In this case, you must obtain an income certification from the prospective tenant, using MDA's form, and execute the lease on MDA's standard lease template. (Both forms can be found on www.mississippi.gov.) All tenants must have eligible incomes at or below 120% of AMI, and you must rent the majority of units (if more than two) to tenants with incomes at or below 80% of AMI.

Required Paperwork

To apply for the SRAP forgivable loan, the following forms must be completed as part of the Small Rental Assistance Program Financing Plan (forms are available at www.mississippi.gov or at www.mda.gov):

- MDA Small Rental Assistance Program Application, which includes:
  - Eligibility information
  - Contact person information
  - Site information
  - Mortgage information
  - Individual/Primary owner information
  - Business entity information
  - Co-owner information (if applicable)
  - Information for each prospective rental unit (home)

- Income and Expense Analysis, which includes:
  - Current rental income
  - Property expenses
  - Five-year operating pro forma (rental income minus expenses)

- Financing Plan, which includes:
  - Property information
  - Existing debt obligations
  - Other financing for the property
  - Sources and use of funds

- Marketing Plan: how you intend to maintain tenant occupancy during the five-year period.

- Management Plan: how you will responsibly manage the property.

In addition to the application and other forms I mentioned, you must include the following documents when applying:

- Consent for Non-Public Personal Information Release Form (included in the application), signed by each owner, co-owner, director, or principal named on the application.

- Copy of the warranty deed or other documents establishing site control of the property.

- Personal financial statement.

- Organizational documents for corporations, LLCs, and partnerships (Articles of Incorporation, LLC, Agreements, or Partnership Agreements).

- Evidence that the business entity is in good standing to transact business in Mississippi.

If you choose to invest in the GO Zone through us, build a home on the lots we have secured, and/or select A-Shore-Bet Property Management, LLC, to manage your property and home, our qualified experts will assist you in every step of the Small Rental Assistance Program application process. You'll secure the forgivable loan financing, which, when added to down payment financing through the Tonja Demoff Foundation (should you exercise that option), will enable you to carry a lending institution mortgage of as low as $109,000 on a $165,000 home, leaving fully one-third of the home's equity outside the walls of the lending institution. The great thing about this? If you qualify for and exercise all of this GO Zone financing, you still haven't paid any hard cash!

From there, it's up to the builder to construct your home, and the GO Zone is packed with incentives for builders as well.

CHAPTER

10

For the Builder

New construction is hopping in the GO Zone at a pace and volume parts of the Deep South haven't seen in thirty years! Local builders are so swamped with commercial, industrial, and residential projects that a golden opportunity exists for outside builders to participate in this massive rebuilding effort, which stretches over more than one hundred counties in five states.

"The contractors out there have more work lined up than they can handle, and a lot of it is due to the GO Zone tax incentives," Perry Nations, director of workers' compensation and legislative services for the Associated General Contractors of Mississippi, told the *Mississippi Business Journal.* "They are absolutely swamped with work. They want to be swamped with work."

The two primary incentives of the GO Zone Act—tax-exempt bonds and the 50 percent bonus depreciation—are driving business and private investors into the GO Zone to such a degree that outside builders are needed to keep up with demand. And there is great demand: In Mississippi alone, 70,000 homes were lost to Hurricane Katrina. In the entire GO Zone, the number is close to 300,000 homes.

As Nations told the *Mississippi Business Journal*, "I see this boom continuing for three, four or five more years, especially when you tie it in with public construction. Contractors are in for extremely good times in the next five to 10 years."

The boom is stretching across the entire construction industry, from services to equipment sectors. With much of the preexisting inventory purchased after Hurricane Katrina for cleanup purposes, numerous equipment lease and rental businesses have sprouted up in the past two years. This has made it possible for out-of-state builders to set up shop without an undue amount of overhead and equipment inventory, and the associated upkeep and maintenance costs. Consequently, out-of-state builders can run lean, efficient operations and align themselves with specific interests and ongoing projects within the GO Zone, such as our large developments in Hancock County.

This is where you, the builder, come in. Below, I'd like to share some of the ways in which you can relocate operations or send crews to the GO Zone states and participate in this phenomenal rebuilding of the Gulf Coast, and take advantage of the services and programs we offer.

The Need for Homes

The current peak need for homes on the Gulf Coast is being pushed by a number of factors that include:

- The tax and investment incentives connected to the GO Zone Act.

- Local residents trying to move out of apartments, FEMA trailers, and other temporary housing through various renter assistance programs.

- Recovery and rebuilding of basic infrastructure and businesses in the hardest-hit areas has progressed to the point that old and new residents alike are attracted to the Gulf Coast and want to get in soon.

- FEMA's plans to remove all remaining trailers from the GO Zone, which will create another wave of demand for homes.

Post Properties for Sale

On our website, www.thegozoneconnection.com, we provide you the opportunities to post properties you're selling. Simply click the "Builders Only" button, and fill out the short form that will enable you to post properties on the website; it will also help us represent your properties.

Our Focus: Modular Homes

Our primary new construction focus in the GO Zone lies in the developments we control and manage, Waveland and Shore Acres. Between the two, we're rolling up our sleeves and undertaking quite a task: erecting nearly 15,000 beautiful modular homes in a short period of time. We're signing up new investors every day, and they want to take advantage of the tax breaks, bonus depreciation, and investment opportunities afforded by the GO Zone Act and other programs.

Thus, we're working at warp speed to erect houses, which leads us to modular homes. Because our manufacturing partners, Safeway Homes and Oak Creek Homes, can turn out three homes per day from their factories during this time of heightened demand, we can assure builders that they can assemble the components on site in a very short period of time. I like to assure our investors that, from the time they close, we can have their three- or four-bedroom single family unit or duplex in place in three to four weeks, as opposed to an average of nine months for stick-built houses.

The beauty of working with modular homes is manyfold. In chapter 7, I shared with prospective investors the general advantages of modular homes over stick-built construction. To the builder, the advantages are even more obvious:

- The homes are delivered to the site in their component parts. They only need to be assembled.

- Homes come in set floor plans, requiring little finish work.

- Homes can be completed in a very short period of time, enabling builders to rotate to the next project quickly.

- Homes can be assembled by small crews of, for example, a foreman and one or two workers. There is no need to carry large payrolls. Swiftness and efficiency are the goals.

- Our incentive-sharing program is such that the builder's profit amounts to an average of $10,000 to $12,000 per single-family unit. If you're a small contractor assembling five to seven units a month, those numbers stack up nicely!

- States offer insurance discounts and incentives for builders in the GO Zone. In Mississippi, for example, builders receive two years of free insurance!

Your Part of the Application Process

Part of the investor's application process for the MDA's Small Rental Assistance Program's loan package, or the "forgivable loan," involves you, the builder. The application package is required to include a contractor's estimate for the home. Because we're primarily working with modular homes delivered by Safeway Homes and Oak Creek Homes, the paperwork will be far more streamlined than usual.

However, it is important for you to know what is required on the standard contractor's estimate form:

- Property observation

- Scope of construction/reconstruction

- Interior and exterior plans

- Detailed work write-up, with an average cost per unit and a total cost for each item

Home Specifications and Features

Manufactured by Safeway Homes and Oak Creek Homes (see chapter 7), the modular homes we offer to investors in the GO Zone meet not only the specifications laid out by the Mississippi Development Authority, but also those mandated by a variety of applicable codes. They include the Southern Building Code Congress International Standard for Hurricane Resistant Residential Construction (SSTD 10), Minimum Design Load for Buildings and Other Structures (ASCE-7), and the international residential, mechanical, plumbing, electrical, and building codes. In addition, our homes are fully covered by a warranty underwritten by Bonded Builders Warranty Group.

The specifications for the homes we offer are more extensive and demanding than other site-built homes. Let's compare.

Our Modular Home Standard Features:

- Structural solid concrete slab foundation
- R-19 insulated 2" × 10" treated floor joist
- Prewired telephone/high speed Internet/cable TV
- Whole house water cut off in the utility room
- Walk-in closets in all bedrooms, with lights
- Sheetrock is hot-glued to studs and rafters (no nail heads to remove later)
- 9" marriage wall for superior strength
- 1 3/4" insulated exterior doors
- 2" × 6" exterior studs
- Exterior studs are glued and fastened with 4" screws to floor system
- Eight steel straps are bolted to the concrete slab and lagged to 2"×6" studs (patent pending)
- Treated 2" × 8" sill is bolted to slab
- Steel plates attach home to the 2" × 8" treated sill and to the 2" × 10" treated floor joist at 2' o. c. (patent pending)
- R-21 rated exterior walls
- Low "E" insulated vinyl windows with screens
- 7/16" OSB is glued and fastened with 3 1/2" screws to exterior studs on all eight sides
- Continuous house wrap vapor barrier
- R-38 blown cellulose insulation in the attic
- 15/32" OSB roof deck with radiant barrier
- 30 lb. roof felt
- 30-year architectural asphalt shingle roof
- Ridge vent for superior attic ventilation
- Inclement weather never touches the inside of your home
- Walls are built in a perfectly square and level jig
- Superior component materials are purchased in truck-load quantities for maximum savings
- Material pilferage is zero and waste is at a minimum
- Move into your new home in only three to five days
- Approved for all available financing
- Home warranty by Bonded Builders Warranty Group
- Structurally rated for over 160 mph winds

Features of a Typical Site-Built House

- Structurally solid concrete slab foundation
- Concrete slab not insulated
- Prewired for telephone
- Whole house water cut-off at the street meter
- Walk-in closet in owner's bedroom
- Sheetrock is nailed to studs and ceiling rafters
- 4" Interior walls
- 1 3/4" insulated exterior doors
- 2"× 4"exterior studs
- Exterior studs are only nailed to bottom plate and top plate
- Steel strap innovation (patent pending) not available to site builders

- Treated 2" × 4" sill is bolted to slab
- 2" × 4" studs are usually only nailed to sill plate

- R-11 rated exterior walls
- Usually insulated without low "E" feature
- 7/16" OSB is nailed as corner bracing and insulation board is used as a filler

- Continuous house wrap vapor barrier
- R-30 blown or batt insulation in the attic
- 7/16" OSB roof deck (radiant barrier optional)
- 15 lb. Roof felt
- 20-year asphalt shingle roof
- Optional feature
- Open air construction is at the mercy of the weather
- Walls are built on site with hand tools
- Numerous trips by different suppliers to the job site delivering material

- Pilferage and waste is always a problem
- Usually takes three to four months to site build
- Approved for all available financing
- Similar warranties
- Typical rating is between eighty to hundred mph winds

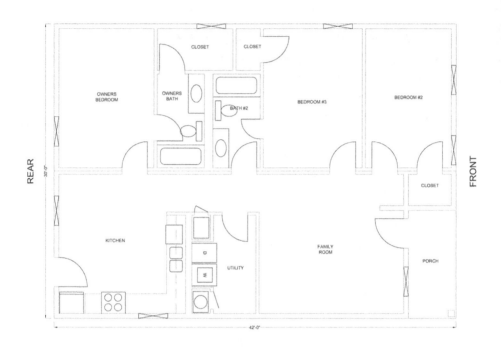

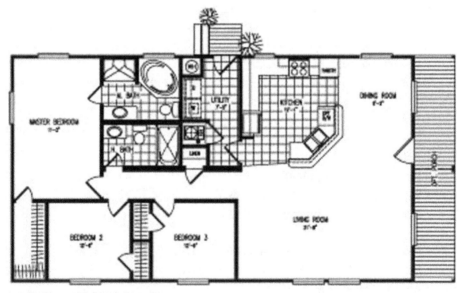

MODEL 8051-PORCH-MOD
28' X 55'
1366 SQ. FT. (PORCH AREA NOT INCLUDED)
3 BEDROOMS, 2 BATHS

CHAPTER

11

The Future Gulf Coast Market

I'd like to share with you an economic reality that would thrill any investor or banker: the entrepreneurial spirit is alive and well. Small business is skyrocketing. Big business is relocating to new head-quarters and factories. Construction starts are booming. New jobs are appearing every day. The unemployment rate is plummeting. Community revitalization has never been better. Tourism is again booming. Is it just me, or does this picture jump out at you, too?

Welcome to the Gulf Coast, circa 2008. Less than three years removed from the devastation wrought by Hurricane Katrina, the Gulf Coast has not only bounced back with a flourish, but is gener-ating an economic recovery that promises to make the area a Mecca for large and small businesses, residents, investors, and tourists for the foreseeable future.

When I think about investing in a property for which I would like to see appreciable growth in market value, one of my first questions is always this: what does the current and future economic growth picture look like?

In the past year, this question hasn't always produced answers that would be considered good news in America. Part of being what I like to call a quantum investor, one who is willing to move his or her assets toward the greatest possible opportunities, is to shift resources into marketplaces on the upswing. And there are very few marketplaces with greater upsides right now than the Gulf Coast, in particular the GO Zone.

Not only is the Gulf Coast booming with new construction, revitalized communities, and the presence of new and expanding business interests, but it's also quickly picking up a reputation as a national "hot spot" in which to set up shop. This point was made by Dean from Michigan in an interview, which appears on the GO Zone video we produced and presented on our website, www.the-gozoneconnection.com. "I can tell you that Mississippi as a state was not a state people were hearing a lot about before the storm," he said. "It's a state that really had a chance to show the country what it could do. Now it's a state that's doing phenomenally well. Governor [Haley] Barbour is doing a spectacular job of leading the recovery and selling Mississippi in terms of an economic place to do development and bring your jobs. Already, Toyota and GE have brought new plants to the state."

Now it's a state that's doing phenomenally well. Take that statement, then add to it projections made by leading construction officials on how the boom times may last for the next decade or more, and you will see what I see: a chance to invest in an area that is going to experience strong market value appreciation and economic prosperity. What/who are the drivers for this boom? They are the outside private and corporate investors, incentivized state and federal packages that include the GO Zone Act, and state programs in

Louisiana, Mississippi, Alabama, Texas, and Florida, with Mississippi's various incentives being particularly progressive.

What also impresses me is the opportunities that entrepreneurs are seeing in places where, a few years ago, they never would have considered investing. When President Bush visited Bay St. Louis on August 29, 2007, to commemorate the two-year anniversary of Katrina, he cited local businesswoman Kay Goff. Kay was the first person to start a new business in downtown Bay St. Louis post-Katrina. She opened a bookstore. "She recognizes the uniqueness of the community, she's a lifelong reader, and she's concerned about what happened to the community," the president said in comments carried live on CNN. "It's an interesting example of the entrepreneurial spirit combined with a [sense of] civic duty." [7]

That spirit has been facilitated by leaders such as Mississippi Governor Haley Barbour and Bay St. Louis Mayor Eddie Favre, both role models of the post-Katrina spirit of innovation, opportunity creation, and optimism. Consequently, the entire area has been energized. Let's also not forget retired Senator Trent Lott, the architect of the GO Zone Act.

A vital point when considering a home investment in the GO Zone that cannot be overstated is this spirit of recovery. Whenever you combine entrepreneurial spirit and skill, well-used incentive packages, a customer base in an improving job market, and a sense of community, you're going to have an area that thrives economically. It is in places like these that economic engines tend to accelerate for a long period of growth, and where an investment, especially a new home, appreciates handsomely.

---

7 Rush Transcript, "Gulf Coast Residents Reflect on Two Years Since Katrina," comments by President George W. Bush, CNN, Aug. 29, 2007.

Impressive Economic Indicators

When you present a snapshot of the significant economic indicators to an incoming homebuyer, together with the outlook in Mississippi, you see get impressive scenarios such as the following:

- Job growth will continue for the next several years through small business development, relocation of corporate interests to the area, and new construction. In fact, employment levels have been above pre-Katrina figures for nearly a year.

- Unemployment rates are dropping nearly every month. By summer 2007, the three coastal counties of Hancock, Harrison, and Jackson had an average unemployment rate of 6.1%, well below the state average of 6.9%. As of February 2008, that average had fallen to 5.8%.

- Sales tax revenues are setting records in several municipalities along the coast.

- The GO Zone is an upswing market in a generally weak economic time, and it is, therefore, an ideal place to invest. Forecasts call for a 15% annual appreciation of home prices.

- The population base in the hardest-hit areas is now as high as 99% of what is was pre-Katrina, and is expected to surpass the 100% pre-Katrina figures.

- New casinos, hotels, and beachfront high-rise condominiums are rising throughout the Gulf Coast, enticing tourists who will pour billions annually into the region.

- New commercial and industrial development is at a 30-year high, according to the Associated General Contractors of Mississippi.

The Nation's Newest Economic Powerhouse: Mississippi

Our two biggest development offerings are located in Mississippi, the nation's newest economic powerhouse. Governor Barbour and his staff have been tremendously successful in convincing new businesses to relocate to the state, including Hancock County, where our primary developments are located. "Many companies have chosen to locate and create jobs in Mississippi because they liked what they saw in our response to Katrina," the governor wrote in *Hurricane Katrina Two Years Later*, the official report from his office on statewide progress. "The country has given our state a second look since the storm, and that's a main reason our future is so promising."[8]

I'd like to point to several features in this report that illustrate why, if you purchase a home in the Mississippi GO Zone, you're going to be reaping the fruits of an escalating market for years to come:

- In March 2007, Governor Barbour signed the Mississippi Growth and Redevelopment Act of 2007, which provided sought-after relief for small businesses faced with skyrocketing insurance premiums. This act is widely credited for igniting the small business growth that has since taken place, as owners had more dollars to invest in inventory, advertising, and marketing.

- Also in March 2007, Governor Barbour signed legislation to allow more small- and mid-sized businesses to qualify for GO

---

8 "Hurricane Katrina Two Years Later," Official Report of Mississippi Governor's Office, Aug. 29, 2007, page 1.

119

Zone tax-exempt bond financing of between $350,000 and $4 million to use for the expansion or building of new facilities. Previously, only industrial and manufacturing projects were eligible, but the legislation, House Bill 1390, enabled most commercial businesses—including retail and service-related businesses, the crucial sources of consumer-based economic growth—to participate.

- The Mississippi Development Authority (MDA) allocated more than $150 million in grants for downtown revitalization programs, enabling local governments to rebuild and repair structures in nineteen municipalities in the lower six counties, including Hancock County.

- The MDA also allocated $10 million for local governments to use to create comprehensive land use and zoning plans, which are road maps to prosperous futures.

- The MDA is moving, through applications, to award $340 million in economic development infrastructure grants, and to attract new industries and the well-paying jobs that come with them.

- With beaches clean and fully restored, the summer 2007 hotel room occupancy on Mississippi's coast reached 63% of pre-Katrina levels, with almost 11,000 rooms in operation. The forecast for summer 2008 is to top 80% of pre-Katrina levels; within five years, it is expected that hotel room occupancy will exceed pre-Katrina rates.

The Long-term Driving Force: The Private Sector

Who will continue to fuel the economic powerhouse that much of the GO Zone is becoming? The people who stand to contribute and also benefit most from it, people like you and me, who comprise the private sector.

"The private sector is the engine that will drive Mississippi's long-term recovery," said Gulf Coast Business Council President Brian Sanderson in *Hurricane Katrina Two Years Later*. "Hurricane Katrina has presented unique economic opportunities for our state."[9]

The private sector has pumped money into the area through its three main actors: big businesses, small businesses, and new homebuyers. In Hancock County alone, where our Waveland and Bay St. Louis offerings are located, Rolls-Royce is building a new outdoor jet-testing facility at the John C. Stennis Space Center; and PSL-North America, one of the largest spiral pipe manufacturing companies in the world, is constructing a pipe manufacturing and coating facility on 155 acres in the Port Bienville Industrial Park. The plant will initially employ 275 people at annual wages averaging $50,000 per year.

Existing industries are also prospering. Gaming and entertainment concerns, heavily damaged by Katrina, are now reporting record revenues. The single largest post-Katrina investment on the Mississippi coast, Harrah's Margaritaville Casino & Resort, is under construction. Finally, small businesses are sprouting up by the thousands, along with support businesses that had no reason

---

9 Ibid., p. 9.

to exist three years ago—for example, the construction equipment rental and leasing centers.

As you can see, everything is in place for many years of prosperity in the GO Zone. And don't forget: where there is growing prosperity, increasing home ownership, higher median incomes, and lower unemployment, there is often double-digit annual appreciation on home values.

That's the kind of economic future every investor should seek.

CHAPTER

12

Warning Signs: What to Watch Out For

Like any great investment opportunity, the GO Zone involves a variety of individuals, lenders, contractors, realtors, and property management concerns—some credible, some not.

It's very important to take a scrupulous, common-sense approach as you invest in the GO Zone. You must be certain that the people you work with have your best interests at heart, that they are highly qualified, and that they possess impeccable credibility. In addition, you need to be sure that the home in which you've invested is built on the lot you chose, with the features and specs you were promised.

I would say this to anyone preparing to invest a large sum of money, whether it be in a home, retirement plan, business, or other financial ventures: Enter the process with eyes wide open, do your homework, and ask good questions. Know what you're getting into, and be sure that you have confidence in the team that is working on your behalf.

Below is a list of key things to consider before investing in the GO Zone:

Appraisals:

In any upward market, such as the GO Zone, appraisals are determined by the purchase price. Be careful of overbuying.

Realtor and Property Management Company:

Work with a credible company that has an office in the GO Zone, and physically touch the property you're going to buy. (See chapter 8.)

Pre-Construction Property:

Understand the differences between stick-built homes, modular homes, and manufactured homes. Understand the differences in features, time to build, and protection against severe weather, such as hurricanes. Learn to speak the language of the builder.

Lots:

If you order a duplex, and the county ordinance says the duplex must sit back from the lot line, and the lot barely meets minimum size requirements, then you're looking at a zero lot line—which means you will be without a yard. Make sure the builder provides you with exact dimensions of your lot, and that your lot has space for a yard (if you so desire). Also, question the lot-specification guidelines for corner properties, the size of which, because of their angular dimensions, could be fudged to your disadvantage. Make sure the size works for you.

Understand Property Guidelines:

Before giving the green light to a builder to proceed, or having your realtor give the builder the go-ahead, make sure you understand the guidelines of your property and home. Don't rely on the builder to tell you if it qualifies or not; know the specifications yourself. The builder has no responsibility.

Licensing:

Make sure your contractor has the proper license, and that it's current and in good standing. We provide a link to reputable builders and their license numbers (and states) on our website, www.thegozoneconnection.com.

See the Property:

Beware of real estate agents who talk to you on the phone or by email and tell you something like, "You don't need to worry; I'll send you photos of the property." Go see the property yourself. As I mentioned earlier in this book, if you can invest $165,000 or $200,000 for a home, you can spend a few hundred dollars on a plane ticket to visit the property you're considering.

Know the Team:

Know who is involved in your GO Zone investment at every step of the process. Research and become familiar with your realtor, the manufacturer (if you're buying a modular home), the builder, and the property management company. If you work with us, we keep the process simple and entirely transparent. We also provide builder license information (as noted) and links to our home manufacturers on our website, www.thegozoneconnection.com.

Earnest Money Deposits:

This issue is especially important. If you're working with a financially stable builder, that company will not need your hard cash to buy the lot on which your home will sit. When you make your nonrefundable earnest money deposit, make it to your real estate agent, not your builder. The agent has your best interest in mind, because he or she receives no commission unless the sale is complete. The builder does not have your best interest in mind; the company simply wants to build the home and get paid. Furthermore, I contend that builders who need earnest money deposits to get the ball rolling are financially unstable and can thus jeopardize your investment, or make you to lose it entirely.

Builders:

Exercise due diligence and know your building team. Learn about the manufacturer and the contractor. Because Mississippi, for example, only tests contractor licenses twice per year, many out-of-state or even in-state builders work in the GO Zone under the licenses of other contractors. Here are some questions to ponder upon:

- Does your builder hold a Mississippi contractor's license? Or is your builder working under someone else's license? Although this is certainly legal, such loop holes do increase the need for you to perform due diligence on the building team.

- Does your builder hold appropriate insurance?

- Does your builder have financial stability? For example, we do not release buyers' earnest-money deposits to builders, because they should be financially stable enough to build your home without them.

- Does your builder have a solid reputation for completing projects in areas outside their home locales?

For our part, we only work with reputable builders who come to us with high recommendations and have met our strict standards. It is a very important form of advocacy that we provide to you.

Insurance:

Make sure you understand the specific homeowner insurance requirements for your home's location. Look especially at two things: requirements specific to the state, and requirements related to hurricanes. The post-Katrina mess in Louisiana, Mississippi, and Alabama should remind you of the importance of knowing the details of your homeowner's policy. The issue post-Katrina boiled down to a simple question: Was the home destroyed/damaged by the act of the hurricane (storm surge, winds, rains)? Or did it fall victim to the post-Katrina flood, specifically the levee breaks in New Orleans? Many thousands of homeowners suffered complete uncompensated losses because their insurance provided hurricane or flood coverage, but not both. *Acts of God*, to use the term, are tricky areas in homeowner policies. Make sure your policy provides coverage for both hurricane and flood. We work only with insurers who cover both.

When you make your GO Zone investment through a highly reputable realty and property management company with deep knowledge of the market and a strong network of locally based builders, such as the company we operate, many of your concerns will disappear. However, I recommend that you always choose to learn the details and the plusses and potential minuses of your investment. Become fully knowledgeable, and you will put yourself in a position to reap the greatest benefit. This leads me to my final words of caution: beware of the person who appeals to your very busy life and perceived lack of R&R (research and review) time by telling you, "I can handle it all for you. Just send the money, do nothing else, and we'll build your home."

I would never send a check to such a person, nor should you. That is one of the reasons I wrote this book. I want you to know the ins and outs of your GO Zone investment as you prepare to do business with us and capitalize on this magnificent opportunity.

CHAPTER

13

What Happens if Another Hurricane Hits?

Your nonowner occupied home is bustling with activity. Your tenants are completely immersed in their lives, grateful to be living in a nice home again and looking forward to the day when they can exercise the option to buy the home from you. Your home sits in a scenic low-lying locale where recovery and new development are booming; you can practically close your eyes and see the property appreciation climbing. It's summer, the Gulf Coast is teeming with vacationing tourists basking in the heat, and your investment home is a source of happiness and opportunity.

Then you flick on The Weather Channel to see how the day looks to take out your sailboat or yacht to Newport Beach—or Newport, Rhode Island—and the words on the screen stop you: *SPECIAL REPORT: Hurricane Bears Down on Gulf Coast*

Not again, you think. *Those people are going to face another potential disaster!*

A second later, another thought hits you: *What about my home or homes down there?*

It's a worthy concern, especially considering that the majority of homes destroyed or damaged by Hurricanes Katrina, Rita, and Wilma did not receive insurance compensation equal to their appraised value. In hundreds of thousands of cases, homeowners lost everything due to under-insurance or the fact they sank their life savings into the home and its monthly mortgage payments, whether on an ARM or fixed mortgage.

Moreover, you're an advance planner; you foresee the eventuality of a future hurricane as you contemplate investing in a home or homes within the GO Zone. It's not hard to imagine. We've experienced a highly active hurricane cycle for the past sixteen years, dating back to Hurricane Andrew. The four-year period between 2003 and 2006 was the most active; it effectively changed the population base as well as the look of the Gulf Coast from Galveston to Key West as we knew it.

OK, you say. *Wait a minute. Maybe I should think twice about this GO Zone home investment, no matter how remarkable the tax incentives and Gulf Coast housing market.* I hear your concerns. I hear them every day from the investors, contractors, insurance agents, lenders, and Gulf Coast residents.

I also have some good news for you: *your home investment and your cash position will both be in great shape if another major hurricane roars through.* Due to the timing of incentives and the strict requirements the GO Zone Act and state programs place on insurance coverage for all homes built or repaired, in part, by government loans, you as the homeowner are well covered.

Let's assume the next big hurricane hits within five years of your purchase(s), and your home(s) suffer either complete destruction or major damage. Already, for a hard cash outlay that could be as low as zero—that is, if you took advantage of all the financing opportunities—you have received:

- The 50% bonus depreciation allowance from the IRS—an $82,500 direct deduction from your adjusted gross income, assuming your home cost $165,000. You've also received annual 3.64% depreciation allowances for each year you owned the home.

- The Small Rental Assistance Program's forgivable loan, a total of up to $40,000 paid toward construction of the home. Assuming you've complied with its terms, the loan is considered forgiven in the event of another natural disaster within the GO Zone.

- You're well insured for both hurricane and flood, so your insurance will cover all damages (minus the deductible); it will compensate the lender in the event of total destruction.

- You've received regular rental payments from your tenants, off-setting your mortgage in a near zero-zero cash neutral manner.

- You've built up equity in the home.

If the hurricane were to hit more than five years after you built the home or homes, your position would be even stronger:

- The SRAP loan would be completely forgiven.

- Under terms of the GO Zone program, you've sold the home to the tenant at current market value at the time of sale, thereby enjoying all of that profit.

- You've received every other incentive connected with the program.

Thus, your investment and your cash position are well protected, no matter what the weather does in any given year.

I've seen and participated in countless real estate transactions for residents, large and small businesses, commercial properties, hotel/resort properties, and more. In my twenty years in the business, I can assure you that I have never seen a nonowner occupied home investment package like that provided by the GO Zone Act. The powers that be in the GO Zone states, along with the federal government, have turned to the private sector to drive the long-term rebuilding of the Gulf Coast with this absolute diamond of an act. They have done their level best to make sure private investors participate in a program that rewards them handsomely for their financial commitment, aids moderate-income local residents who need a foothold—and a home—to reclaim their lifestyles and their future plans, and fuels the Gulf Coast's recovery from the devastating triple whammy of Katrina, Rita, and Wilma.

When I look at the GO Zone today and its rebuilding projects, the homeowner in me relishes the beauty and style of the new homes. The philanthropist in me feels deeply warmed by the gratefulness of local residents who've been given another chance by an outside investor's decision. The real estate agent in me sees years of booming economy and market prosperity. The real estate investment strategist in me sees a tremendous way for my clients to generate more income, fund education plans, bolster their real estate portfolios, and set themselves up for retirement. And, finally, the investor in me knows that, in my lifetime, I may never see a home-buying package so filled with incentives and market-growth potential as the one I've described in this book.

This is where you come in. This is where you get into the Gulf Zone Opportunity Act.

Join us!

APPENDIX A:

The GO Zone Connection

Our official GO Zone website, www.thegozoneconnection. com, is a rich online community, with information, links, and other resources and tools that will further help you learn more about the incredible investment opportunity of owning a home, or a group of homes, in the Gulf Opportunity Zone. Among the many features you will find at www. thegozoneconnection.com are the following:

- Background information and history of Hurricanes Katrina, Rita, and Wilma; the GO Zone; and the GO Zone Act.

- Pictures of the GO Zone.

- Audio and video interviews of business owners, government officials, and residents of the GO Zone.

- GO Zone benefits.

- GO Zone frequently asked questions.

- Direct links to printable PDF files of IRS Publication 4492 ("Information for Taxpayers Affected by Hurricanes Katrina, Rita and Wilma"); and the Mississippi Small Rental Assistance Program Application Guidebook, which are the central components of the home investment program.

- Links to Safeway Homes and Oak Creek Homes, our modular home-manufacturing partners.

- Link to A-Shore-Bet Property Management, LLC, our property management center based in Bay St. Louis, Mississippi.

- Source list of builders working in the GO Zone, good and bad, and the status of their licenses.

- Flowchart that shows the process of buying a home through us.

- Features, specifications, pictures, descriptions, and floor plans of modular homes we offer.

- Information and registration for GO Zone tours.

- Information and registration for GO Zone investment seminars.

- Investors network for information sharing.

- Online property purchase feature that includes:
  - Property selection
  - Prequalification for loan
  - Purchase agreement submission
  - Initial deposit through secure transaction
  - Online signatures
  - Open escrow

ALSO FROM

Tonja Demoff

Bubble Proof:

Real Estate Strategies that Work in any Market

With the techniques and insider's secrets that she has used during her astonishing career, Tonja Demoff provides a formula for success and profit in any market and in any financial situation, whether you're investing in your first house or your fiftieth. Tonja has succeeded by investing wisely in single-family homes and multi-units that doubled, tripled, even quadrupled her money. And Tonja shows why the housing market is poised to rise for years to come, taking smart investors along on the ride to even greater profit and financial security.

In *Bubble Proof*, you'll learn to:

- Overcome fear and move toward a better financial future
- Understand the laws of making money and have them work for you

- Learn dozens of ways to structure and finance great deals

- Create market opportunities to maximize return on investment

- Decide whether to go for cash flow or speculation when investing

- Stay motivated in a roller-coaster economy so you always come out ahead

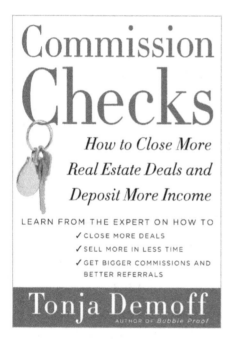

Commission Checks:

How to Close More Real Estate Deals and Deposit More Income

Commission Checks provides real estate professionals with tested and proven expertise to improve prospecting, buying, selling, and profiting in today's complex real estate market. It explains author Tonja Demoff's innovative techniques for selling more real estate in less time, with bigger commissions and better referrals. It's the system Tonja created and followed to success time and again.

In *Commission Checks*, readers will discover:

- Why hands-on real estate agent training doesn't exist, and how to overcome a lack of experience and start selling now

- How to uncover hidden options and strategies that lead to sales

- Why educating clients about the market is a powerful sales tool

- Why there's no such thing as a soft market

- How to overcome fear of failure and become more productive almost overnight

The Casual Millionaire:

Wealth by Intention

The Casual Millionaire uncovers the true secrets to becoming happy and unleashing the hidden money-making machine inside us all. How can the act of becoming happy possibly make you millions? Author Tonja Demoff is living proof that being happy will be a major factor in creating greater wealth in America. Her philosophy is supported by a recent RAND Corporation study, which found that those who reported excellent well-being nearly doubled their household wealth over a decade. In contrast, folks whose well-being declined over the decade lost money. In this book, Tonja reveals her secrets to unlocking the happy millionaire we all dream of being.

ABOUT THE AUTHOR

Tonja Demoff

Investing in the Go Zone author Tonja Demoff shares her personal experiences of success with real estate investors throughout the country. She constantly looks for opportunities that will benefit others as well as herself, and, in her estimation, few opportunities have been as rich with promise as the Gulf Opportunity Zone.

Tonja has founded more than ten companies. She became successful while inspiring thousands of people to take action, experience results, and live up to their true potential. Her personal story is truly moving. She went from being flat broke to being one of America's highest-paid realtors, earning the prestigious rank as the number 1 ReMax real estate agent in the United States in 2007.

She was placed into the ReMax Hall of Fame after just one year as a realtor, and she has maintained her status as the top real estate agent for ReMax in College Park Realty in Southern California. She also continues to earn the Chairman's Club and Platinum Club honors.

As an entrepreneur in real estate and motivational speaking for the past eighteen years, Tonja founded the Tonja Demoff Foundation, which actively funds programs for low-income homebuyers and underwrites numerous community projects. She is a sought-after lecturer, instructor, and consultant.

Tonja is the author of three other books: *The Casual Millionaire: Wealth by Intention; Bubble Proof: Real Estate Strategies That Work in Any Market; and Commission Checks: How to Close More Real Estate Deals and Deposit More Income.* She has also created seven CD/ DVD educational packages, including: *First-Time Home Buyers Boot Camp, Believe & Achieve, Credit Repair Secrets, Partnering For Profits, The Real Estate Millionaire Mindset, Quantum Cash™ Program, and Financial Freedom Seminar System.* While seeking to launch a regional television show, she recently launched *Quantum Cash*, a national infomercial series.

FREE BONUS!

The GO Zone Opportunity Webinar

- Learn more about the Go Zone opportunities

- Determine if the GO Zone opportunity is right for you

- Learn how you can keep more of your income

- Learn about the types of construction in the Go Zone

- View properties that are for sale

- Gain a better understanding of how to have your investment managed

- Learn how you can receive a check for $80,000 before the property even closes

- Learn how your investment creates a home for families in the Go Zone

- Get all your questions answered!

BUY A SHARE OF THE FUTURE IN YOUR COMMUNITY

These certificates make great holiday, graduation and birthday gifts that can be personalized with the recipient's name. The cost of one S.H.A.R.E. or one square foot is $54.17. The personalized certificate is suitable for framing and will state the number of shares purchased and the amount of each share, as well as the recipient's name. The home that you participate in "building" will last for many years and will continue to grow in value.

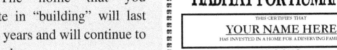

Here is a sample SHARE certificate:

HABITAT FOR HUMANITY

THIS CERTIFIES THAT
YOUR NAME HERE
HAS INVESTED IN A HOME FOR A DESERVING FAMILY

1985-2005
TWENTY YEARS OF BUILDING FUTURES IN OUR
COMMUNITY ONE HOME AT A TIME

1200 SQUARE FOOT HOUSE @ $65,000 = $54.17 PER SQUARE FOOT
This certificate represents a tax deductible donation. It has no cash value.

YES, I WOULD LIKE TO HELP!

I support the work that Habitat for Humanity does and I want to be part of the excitement! As a donor, I will receive periodic updates on your construction activities but, more importantly, I know my gift will help a family in our community realize the dream of homeownership. **I would like to SHARE in your efforts against substandard housing in my community!** *(Please print below)*

PLEASE SEND ME _____ SHARES at $54.17 EACH = $ $_____

In Honor Of: _____

Occasion: (Circle One)   HOLIDAY   BIRTHDAY   ANNIVERSARY

       OTHER: _____

Address of Recipient: _____

Gift From: _____   *Donor Address:* _____

Donor Email: _____

I AM ENCLOSING A CHECK FOR $ $_____ PAYABLE TO HABITAT FOR HUMANITY OR PLEASE CHARGE MY VISA OR MASTERCARD *(CIRCLE ONE)*

Card Number _____   Expiration Date: _____

Name as it appears on Credit Card _____   Charge Amount $ _____

Signature _____

Billing Address _____

Telephone # Day _____   Eve _____

PLEASE NOTE: Your contribution is tax-deductible to the fullest extent allowed by law.
Habitat for Humanity • P.O. Box 1443 • Newport News, VA 23601 • 757-596-5553
www.HelpHabitatforHumanity.org